Generous Ecclesiology

enjoy reading

[signature]

*to the best councillor
is the world
with love,
Robert Hayes*

Generous Ecclesiology

Church, World and the Kingdom of God

Edited by
Julie Gittoes, Brutus Green and James Heard

scm press

© The Editors and Contributors 2013

Published in 2013 by SCM Press
Editorial office
3rd Floor
Invicta House
108–114 Golden Lane,
London
EC1Y 0TG

SCM Press is an imprint of Hymns Ancient & Modern Ltd
(a registered charity)
13A Hellesdon Park Road
Norwich NR6 5DR, UK

www.scmpress.co.uk

British Library Cataloguing in Publication data

A catalogue record for this book is available
from the British Library

978-0-334-04662-2

Typeset by Regent Typesetting, London
Printed and bound by
CPI Group (UK) Ltd, Croydon

Contents

Contributors

Jo Bailey Wells is currently Chaplain to the Archbishop of Canterbury.

Jonathan Clark is the Bishop of Croydon in the Diocese of Southwark.

Stephen Conway is the Bishop of Ely.

Julie Gittoes is Residentiary Canon for Education at Guildford Cathedral.

Tom Greggs is Professor of Historical and Doctrinal Theology at the University of Aberdeen and is a local preacher in the Methodist Church.

Brutus Green is Associate Vicar at St John's, Hyde Park in the Diocese of London.

James Heard is Priest-in-Charge, United Benefice of St George Campden Hill and St John the Baptist, Holland Rd.

Ian Mobsby is Priest-in-Charge, Guild Church of St Mary Aldermary, and Missioner to the Moot Community in the Diocese of London.

Jeremy Morris is the Dean Fellow, and Director of Studies in Theology at King's College, Cambridge.

Robert Thompson is Lead Chaplain for the Royal Brompton Hospital and Co-ordinating Healthcare Chaplain in the Diocese of London.

Foreword

JO BAILEY WELLS

God's grace is not in short supply. Its sheer abundance sums up both the reason for this book and the need for it.

There is no doubt that Christians have always struggled to respond to God's grace with the same levels of generosity – most especially to one another. Certainly this is very evident within the Church of England. A culture of scarcity too often predominates – of money, energy, trust or truth – whereby we consider ourselves justified in cutting corners in our vision or strategy (though we likely present it as 'refocusing').

Advocacy groups abound calling for the way in which the Church's vision or strategy might be revised or refocused, often fired by a particular concern. But 'generous ecclesiology' is no such pressure group. Quite the opposite. If there is any sustained campaign behind these chapters it is about overriding all 'issues' for the sake of ensuring that mission serves the Church and the Church serves God. Put in more technical terms, it is about keeping missiology ecclesiological and ecclesiology missiological – the two do not compete or function apart – and maintaining a theological focus to both. In the end, they are only and all about God and God's generous grace – not matters of human pragmatics. The single cause is God, and the single virtue, generosity.

The Church ever stands in need of this reminder. In my own ministry I have long been challenged by a question posed by the eighteenth-century French mystic Charles Péguy: 'When we get to heaven, God will ask: where are all the others?' This is the question that checks my particular passions. It reminds me that the game has little to do with my own passions and convictions. It is not about me. It is about the body – corporate functioning-together – founded on Christ.

If – as in John Milbank's formulation – 'Christianity is the coding of transcendental difference as peace', then it is time to learn how to function together with our differences. Indeed, it is time to learn to enjoy difference, in anticipation of that day of peace when unity will not look like uniformity. We will not sing with the same tune or tongue: instead our voices will form a harmony.

That harmony is the gift of the gospel and the work of the gospel. Paul chooses to describe it with a political term: reconciliation. Seeking harmony or reconciliation does not mean becoming oblivious to difference, ignoring it or overcoming it as if there are no lines to be drawn. It is more like the opposite: it demands that we develop a conflict-resilience that permits us to engage difference in the face of commitment. Sometimes this involves pain; always it will demand patience, persistence and personal relinquishment. Discipleship necessarily involves denying the self, taking up the cross and following Christ.

This book is offered in the hope of shaping church leaders who are theologically focused, mission-minded, ecclesially engaged and conflict-resilient – above all, human beings who are as generous as the God who creates, redeems and calls. That sounds catholic, evangelical and liberal to me.

Introduction

An Invitation to Conversation: Mission and the Church

Over the last decade, mission has claimed the top spot on the agenda of the Anglican Church at a national and local level. In order to respond to the missionary opportunities within contemporary culture, a mixed economy of network churches emerged alongside parishes. However, while the vision for renewal was for the whole Church, not just one wing of it, a dichotomy has emerged. The upsurge in energy and enthusiasm for Fresh Expressions of church has led, in some instances, to feelings of isolation, bewilderment and even hostility for some in traditional parish contexts. It is timely, therefore, to re-engage with a deeper vision of Church and mission, rooted in worship and responsive to the world. Such a vision flows from an understanding of God's generosity. While the mutual suspicion of different parties in the Church can lead to defensive and dismissive withdrawal, it is our belief that the differences that have emerged in relation to mission and ecclesiology demand a generous response.

Mission-Shaped Church (referred to hereafter as *MSC*), published in 2004, is one of the most widely read reports produced by the Church of England.[1] It reflected upon some of the Fresh Expressions of church emerging in response to cultural changes within society and sets out methodologies and frameworks for enabling the Church to proclaim the gospel afresh in this generation. It also sought to set out a theology for a missionary Church – and has generated a plethora of 'mission-shaped'

---

1 *Mission-Shaped Church*, London: Church House Publishing, 2004.

publications, a DVD of inspiring and challenging stories entitled *Expressions: Making a Difference*, and a series of 'Share' booklets to enable parishes to start 'new' churches.

The role of the parish church in Anglican mission, however, was not discussed in detail in the 2004 report. Where it is mentioned, the parish is often seen in negative terms – as being out of date and restrictive, unable to respond to a 'network' society. It has received limited attention in some of the work responding to the report – for example, in *Mission-Shaped Parish* and *The Future of the Parish System*.[2] Yet none of these publications was devoted to a thoroughgoing theological critique of the consequences of Fresh Expressions for our ecclesiology. The collection of essays called *Praying for England*, edited by Sarah Coakley and Sam Wells, affirmed the power of priestly, prayerful presence in the local parish context.[3] However, a sustained conversation is needed if we are to avoid the fragmentation of parish and new churches, and a divided understanding of what it means to be church.

For the Parish (hereafter *FTP*) presented a sharply critical response to *MSC*, and sought to defend the parish church as a locus for mission.[4] In so doing, it acted as a rallying cry and garnered significant support among parish clergy, particularly in the catholic tradition. Its authors remind us that the inherited Church, with its traditions and practices, is not a husk to be discarded in order to retrieve the kernel of the gospel message. They also raise important questions about the relationship between the form of the Church and the faith, and the

2 Steven Croft, *Moving on in a Mission-Shaped Church*, London: Church House Publishing, 2005; Steven Croft (ed.), *The Future of the Parish System: Shaping the Church of England for the 21st Century*, London: Church House Publishing, 2006; John M. Hull, *Mission-Shaped Church: A Theological Response*, London: SCM Press, 2006; Lindsay Urwin (ed.), *Mission-Shaped Questions: Defining Issues for Today's Church*, London: Church House Publishing, 2008; Paul Bayes and Tim Sledge (eds), *Mission-Shaped Parish: Traditional Church in a Changing World*, London: Church House Publishing, 2009; David Goodhew, *Church Growth in Britain*, Ashgate: Farnham, 2012.

3 Sarah Coakley and Sam Wells (eds), *Praying for England*, London: Continuum, 2008.

4 A. Davison and A. Milbank, *For the Parish: A Critique of Fresh Expressions*, London: SCM Press, 2010.

deep-rooted commitment to people and place versus the nature of networks and choice-based communities. Early on, the concept of a 'mixed economy church' is rejected wholesale; yet, in conclusion, the authors acknowledge that in practice there is a relationship to be developed between parishes and Fresh Expressions for mutual benefit.[5]

Reaffirming the possibilities of the parish and its place in the mystery of God's work in the world is vital, but we cannot ignore the challenge of *MSC* in emphasizing the urgent task of engaging in mission in creative and imaginative ways. However, the choice is not an either/or. Davison and Milbank critiqued the idea of a 'mixed economy' church for allowing too much and too little diversity.[6] They went on to conclude, though, that the challenge lies in affirming the connection between inherited patterns of worship and innovative engagements with the missionary task, so that: 'the creativity of the Fresh Expression Pioneers would provoke the parishes to rediscover their innate possibilities for mission. In turn, the parish would provide a grounded community for education and practical discipleship.'[7]

This book seeks to respond to that invitation in order to affirm the connection between inheritance and innovation. It is a response rooted in an exploration of ecclesiology. The Church is not simply a doctrine or idea, but a 'practice of commonality in faith and mission'.[8] The Church is both embedded in God's being and activity and also the embodiment of God's purposes. Its vision flows from the divine source; its calling is to witness to the fulfilment of the kingdom. In anticipation of the *eschaton*, the Church is constituted by worship and mission.

The Church must avoid falsely 'particularizing itself'. If it is to fulfil its doxological calling and missiological task, it must not differentiate itself from the world in ways other than God intends.[9] The Church is not just another 'player' in the

---

5 *FTP*, p. 227.

6 *FTP*, p. 73.

7 *FTP*, pp. 225–7.

8 D. Hardy, *Finding the Church: The Dynamic Truth of Anglicanism*, London: SCM Press, 2001, p. 38.

9 Hardy, *Finding*, p. 38.

world; nor is it an alternative society. The Church's vocation demands both attentiveness to God in worship and also engagement with the world. It is a dynamic body called to share in God's mission in the world. The Church cannot fulfil this call to embody God's purpose apart from worship; nor can the Church be itself if it neglects the call to participate in the world. Therefore, there is no merit in polarizing the debate between an exclusive affirmation of the inherited Church on the one hand and the missionary initiatives taken by the Fresh Expressions movement on the other. It is because the Church is formed by worship that the patterns and structures, in particular the Church's sacramental life, are not to be discarded, or seen as a burden. Likewise, it is because the Church is generated by its mission in the world that being sent out as witnesses is not a second-order activity. Thus this book seeks not to perpetuate a line of argument that becomes oppositional or defensive. Instead, we set out a vision for mission already within the rich diversity of the Anglican tradition, which affirms the witness of all parts of the Church. This affirmation of vision is a response and an invitation to an ongoing conversation.

The Conversation So Far: *Mission-Shaped Church* and *For the Parish*

MSC acknowledged that without the authorized practice of baptism and celebration of the Eucharist, a mission initiative is not yet 'church' as understood by Anglicans. Yet it gave scant attention to the sacramental aspects of the Church's life. This omission cuts the ecclesial body off from the ground of its being. For just as the Church is 'not just another human interest group, so the Eucharist is not just a ritual activity competing for time and space with other religious acts that human beings perform'.[10] The Church, its worship and its mission, are grounded in the social life of the Trinity. It is from the being of God that the Church receives its identity, life and purpose.

---

10 Rowan Williams, 'Theological Resources for Re-examining Church', in Croft (ed.), *The Future of the Parish System*, p. 57.

It is a place of invitation, encounter and commissioning. The Eucharist is where the Church is called into being and where its calling is refreshed. It is a place of nourishment and healing where the community is transformed. The fulfilment of God's kingdom is anticipated in worship; and, by participating in it, the people of God are forgiven, energized and called into service in the world.

MSC talks about the Eucharist in relation to marks of the Church. Having established that an Anglican understanding of Church depends upon the sacraments of baptism and Eucharist, we read the following: churches are eucharistic communities, irrespective of their church tradition, or the frequency of eucharistic worship. The Eucharist lies at the heart of Christian life. It is the act of worship (including the ministry of the Word) in which the central core of the biblical gospel is retold and re-enacted. New expressions of church may raise practical difficulties about authorized ministry, but, if they are to endure, they must celebrate the Eucharist.[11]

This, the main paragraph within the report on the Eucharist, appears to regard the sacrament as both essential and as a potential difficulty. In the light of such a statement it is surprising that the Eucharist does not merit more discussion within the report itself. For if no attempt is made to explore the theology of the Eucharist in relation to mission and what it is to be church, then the fears over practical difficulties will remain. However, it is also an acknowledgement that it is only through the development of sacramental life that Fresh Expressions become 'church'. What starts off as a mission initiative or project grows into an ecclesial community. This raises challenges about what sort of ecclesial community might emerge – is there scope for differences of rhythm and style of worship, while recognizing that patterns of life and witness are being transformed and sustained by an encounter with Christ?

An affirmation of the intensity of such encounters has the potential to deepen appreciation of divine activity in the world, and to acknowledge divine love and grace being made manifest in the other. Churches are eucharistic communities. In the

---

11 *MSC*, p. 101.

hymnody of a non-sacramental denomination, the Salvation Army, we see that this reflects something of the demands of engaging in mission: 'My life must be Christ's broken bread, my love his outpoured wine.'[12] It is perhaps in response to statements about the Eucharist that there emerges some common ground between inherited and emerging churches. Dan Hardy's concept of pre-ecclesial communities is helpful here: it underscores the way in which God is at work in the world, while also affirming the distinctiveness of the Church itself.

Worship itself is fundamentally a corporate activity through which people are embedded into a particular kind of society. The opening words of the liturgy gather those present in the name of God: Father, Son and Holy Spirit. The community shares in the Eucharist and is then sent out in love and peace to love and serve the Lord. But this is more than the formation of a social structure. It is about an encounter with Christ: receiving the gift of his body. As such, the Eucharist is both a place of transformation for the individual and lies at the heart of the Church's mission. The celebration of the Eucharist cannot be fully understood without being attentive to the apostolic imperative at its heart. There is gathering; there is a sending out. Working out the implications of the Eucharist in this way is vital for parishes. It demands the empowerment of the laity, rather than relying on an individual parish priest. It blurs the boundary between Church and world in a way that generously accommodates the spiritually curious or those seeking the Church's blessing in the midst of birth and death and committed relationships.

FTP offers a critique of *MSC* by emphasizing that faith is not just a set of ideas to be understood, but about a way of life located in certain practices. Its authors seek to restore confidence in the parish system. The practices and disciplines of the inherited Church, they rightly assert, should not be seen as just one of many 'styles' of doing and being church: 'The message and purpose of the Church are to be found in the way

---

12 Words taken from a hymn by Albert Osborne (1886–1967), General of the Salvation Army.

she lives and worships.'[13] The book affirms the nature of the Church as given – and reasserts the value of the parish as a given locality over what is chosen within the Fresh Expressions movement. However, there is a risk that the Church's liturgical practices are seen as predetermined and sufficient, leaving the scope of engagement with God's ways in the world limited.

It is all too easy for those within the Church to underestimate the gap between those who attend worship on a regular basis and those living and working within the parish. This gap manifests itself in low-level biblical literacy, unfamiliarity with hymnody, and confusion over liturgical movement. It is also reflected in the reasons given for those seeking infant baptism, marrying in church or requesting that the local vicar conduct a funeral. Often the reasons for these requests are not those anticipated by the Church, or do not neatly fit within the range of theological views of the Church. To say 'yes' in these situations makes demands upon the minister and church community, as we seek to be attentive, to interpret and forge connections. Alan Billings writes of how we are called to listen, understand and respond to such requests in *Secular Lives, Sacred Hearts*. One of the insights of *MSC* is that our awareness of this 'gap' is heightened – not just in relation to the de-churched, but to those who come from a non-church background. Such a perspective is absent from *FTP*. Unless we are able to describe accurately the world within which we live and worship and work, unless we make space to hear the stories and assumptions of those who come to us, we cannot fully engage with the mission of God.

As Tim Jenkins reflects, paying attention to one's context is fundamental to the Anglican vocation. This practice is not a matter of bringing God into a place, but discerning him in it. It is not just about gathering people together, but discovering their desires; what moves them: 'For if God is already present in the world, in particular people and situations, one encounters truth rather than constructing it, and matters of great importance impinge upon one, rather than one's discovering them

---

13 *FTP*, p. 4.

through any act of will or intention.'[14] Part of the Church's vocation is to go to unexpected places. The chaplain and parish priest, the pioneer and the bishop, are charged with this task – but so are the people of God as they are scattered within the world before and after the sacramental interval of gathering for worship.

Being Drawn Deeper in Conversation

Generous ecclesiology is shaped by an understanding of the Church that affirms that worship and the missionary task are non-dualistically bound together. It is rooted in a rich sense of the Anglican tradition, which across theological and liturgical traditions remains committed to the demands of witnessing to the gospel. It rejoices in God's generous love for the world and is attentive to God's activity within it. The Church is called to 'learn how to persist with our task in the world ... Opening up the true potential and resources of human life'.[15] We can only do this by taking liturgy and the world more seriously; by being more attentive to the light of God. A light that is dazzling in its depth; which draws and irradiates, and is refracted in the world.

We are called to be faithful to tradition, yet also open to appropriate innovation. Rowan Williams has written of the weakening of scriptural imagination in our culture and the need for its reinvigoration. The process of interpretation, he writes, is a 'generative moment in which there may be a discovery of what the primal text may become (and so of what it is) as well as a discovery of the world'.[16] These two elements of generation and discovery (or 'finding' and 'fashioning' to use Nicholas Lash's terms) are found frequently in theology to help

---

14 T. Jenkins, *An Experiment in Providence: How Faith Engages with the World*, London: SPCK, 2006, p. 7.

15 D. Hardy, *Wording a Radiance: Parting Conversations on God and the Church*, London: SCM Press, 2010, p. 106.

16 Rowan D. Williams, 'Postmodern Theology and the Judgment of the World', in Frederick B. Burnham (ed.), *Postmodern Theology: Christian Faith in a Pluralist World*, New York: Harper & Row, 2006, pp. 92–112, 94.

uncover what is really the case,[17] and this is no less appropriate with our response to the needs of the Church and the world in ministry and liturgy. New developments in all aspects of the life of the Church will, in different ways, recall us to the original vocation of the Church.

The immediacy of this task is particularly evident in the fluidity of sector ministry. Here we find the necessity of taking the particularity of context seriously, while being mindful of the equal necessity of maintaining a recognizable 'family identity' to established parochial patterns of worship and proclamation, witness and service. The theology and practice of mission cannot be sustained once cut off from the Church's traditional practices and structures, most particularly its sacramental life. Nor is mission an optional extra within the life of the Church; rather, it is intrinsic to its very nature. But in creative moments in the life of the Church, we may find ourselves open to the transcendent presence of God in new ways that extend how we relate to the divine and one another, and help us rediscover what it means to be the holy people of God.

Underlying this assumption lies the conviction that it is the presence of the Eucharist at the heart of the Church's life that holds together patterns of mission, sustains community life and expresses the Church's reliance on the divine initiative. As Rowan Williams expresses it: 'At the moment we probably need a much more robust defence of the supernatural, God-initiated side of our church life and the significance of the sacraments as actually creating the Church week by week.'[18] The Eucharist is central to the way in which the Church proclaims the gospel; it is central to its very being as the body of Christ in and for the world. This is not to diminish the importance of the wider sacramental life of the Church. It is in baptism, for example, that our identities are reconfigured in Christ; that we become part of his body. This is a once and for all event; it is unrepeatable. However, to be sustained in our

---

17 See the discussion of Don MacKinnon's use of Cézanne in Chapter 4 for a fuller discussion of this.

18 Williams, 'Theological Resources for Re-examining Church', p. 60.

discipleship we are to repeatedly 'do this' in remembrance. The presence of Christ in the non-identically repeated sacrament transforms and nourishes the Church. Memory and hope are expressed together, in the present, as the Church is once again scattered in the world. The concept of non-identical repetition takes given patterns seriously as a conduit for the Spirit's activity; yet it also acknowledges the challenge and opportunity of the particular, enabling appropriate improvisation as the Church engages with the world. The Eucharist enables us to think through an ecclesiology that is embodied; formed for and by its worship and mission.

Being drawn deeper into conversation about what it is to embody a generous ecclesiology, rooted in the abundance of God's love, means being attentive to history and context. To that end we offer the following contributions.

From an Anglican point of view, a church is more than a local gathered community based around a particular interest group or style of worship. The role of the bishop in ministry and mission is fundamental to this generous, and universal, understanding of church. Parish clergy share in responsibility for the cure of souls in a particular place, as publicly expressed by the bishop during the service of induction. Both *FTP* and *MSC* leave open questions about the relationship between local mission, ministry and episcopacy. With that in mind, Stephen Conway, in Chapter 1 of this volume, takes this as an area of theological reflection. He explores the diocese as the catholic unit of mission and the local, and the bishop's role in that as a focus not only of unity in ministry, but also unity in mission in multiple contexts, many of which will be supra-parochial or in very different styles. His vision of episcopacy is expansive, apostolic and embedded. He combines an understanding of the bishop as both a defender of faith and focus of unity, with a prophetic calling to Church and culture. This refreshed expression of episcopacy engages with the ministry and mission of Aidan and Cuthbert. In turn, this model is rooted in the pattern of Jesus ministry – of moving onwards through the world, while also withdrawing to pray. Reflections on discipline, authority, leadership, mission and partnership lead into a consideration of the place of holy order for the sake of all God's companions on the way.

This approach offers the opportunity to respond to the challenge of *FTP* by valuing the place of innovation within the catholic tradition; it also responds to the criticism made of *MSC* that it does not take inherited patterns seriously enough. In response, Jeremy Morris (Chapter 2) draws us into the Anglican tradition of social witness in the mid-nineteenth century, a period of rapid social change. He traces the origins of this movement and offers a historical re-description by attending to two of its most influential advocates, F. D. Maurice and Charles Gore. In doing so, he recovers a sense of a profoundly inventive tradition, which is attentive to the building up of Christian community by experimenting with pastoral strategies. The challenge is not only an ecclesial one, but also a corrective to historiography of the Left. Faithfulness to the inheritance of the past enables innovative engagement in the present – inventive mission is the outworking of ecclesiology, 'a tradition of experimentation, out of traditional concerns'. It serves as a reminder that the Church responds to the needs of the world, rooted in mission and worship, and that that vocation has a political and social edge because it is fundamentally concerned with God's ways in the world.

James Heard (Chapter 3) focuses on a particularly missiological theme, inculturation, a term used to refer to the adaptation of the gospel in particular cultures being evangelized. It recognizes that the Christian faith is never transmitted in a culturally neutral cocoon: it needs to be incarnated in the heart of each culture. Inculturation expresses a generous ecclesiology because it lays great stress on being carefully and respectfully attentive to the missional context. It requires being open to seeing the Holy Spirit working in new, perhaps unexpected, places and people and responding creatively. This, quite rightly, was the concern of *MSC*. The other side to cultural context is a concern, expressed in *FTP*, to remain faithful to the riches of Anglican parochial worshipping tradition, and this entails a reflection on ecclesiology. What might fidelity mean for the Anglican tradition? In short, how might the beliefs and practices of a generous missional Church be configured so as to relate continuity and change?

Brutus Green (Chapter 4) seeks to engage with the oppositional and exclusive strands found in some catholic thought today, in particular challenging the prevalent Christendom/ secular–nihilist binary. In *FTP* contemporary culture is written off as consumerist and banal and the medieval period romanticized, which gives way to a defensive authoritarian view of the Church as the place not only of salvation but also of good taste. This chapter seeks instead to develop a positive language of dialogue with contemporary culture, where the Church admits it can learn from the world, without capitulating to its terms entirely and uncritically – a charge that is sometimes levelled at *MSC*. While the Church cannot abandon its ethical and metaphysical integrity, it must also sidestep the post-liberal temptation of radical difference. The challenge is to work towards an engagement that trusts in God's presence in the world and develops an open, inclusive ecclesiology, alive to the Spirit and seeking the kingdom of God where it may be found. Such a model is generous in how it perceives who the body of Christ belongs to, and generous in how it looks for partnerships in mission and service.

Participation in, and the sharing of, the generous love of God is central to the Church's distinctive vocation in a world that is already the arena of God's activity. To understand Church and mission fully means reflecting on the way in which dimensions of human life, in the midst of ever-increasing social complexity, are drawn towards their ultimate fulfilment by God. By active engagement with God's ways in the world, the Church embodies its calling in relation to God's salvific purposes. Thus, Julie Gittoes (Chapter 5) engages with Dan Hardy's conception of a Church called to 'careful walking'. Such dynamic ecclesiology is rooted in worship – being drawn ever more deeply into the very being of God and glimpsing a doxological vision of the fulfilment of God's kingdom. The calling to walking in the world means witnessing to God's activity within it as well as holding that vision. The moving forward in hope foreshadows the fulfilment of God's purpose at the *eschaton*. This wandering and embodied ecclesia is constituted by the Eucharist, which establishes its calling as society – a Church formed by the intensity of worship and the extensity of mission, witnesses to a God of salvation, the limits of whose generous love we cannot identify. To think of our ecclesiology as 'moving' develops the idea of the Church as a pilgrim people on the way. It enables us to speak of healing and provisionality; discipleship and humility.

Any consideration of ecclesiology and mission needs to take account of the ecumenical context. Without this perspective, theology risks becoming sectarian; with it, theological engagement is held within a universal vision of the Church. It takes account of the breadth of our shared tradition; and we learn from the distinctive witness of those sharing in God's generous love. To this end, Tom Greggs (Chapter 6) examines the doctrine of assurance from a Methodist perspective. Writing out of sustained engagement with Wesley's teaching, he critiques notions of false assurance, which fail to recognize Christ's presence in the world. Instead, he argues that assurance of salvation has the capacity to deepen our understanding of a generous ecclesiology as it overflows to love for others in compassion and action, just as God's love embraces the world. The Church needs to become like the sheep in Matthew 25: a people consumed with loving the world, for whom assurance of salvation rests on the Spirit's work and opens up the Church to the present activity of God.

Robert Thompson (Chapter 7) argues that the models of mission offered by MSC and FTP require augmentation in order to offer more flexible engagement both with other Christians and with people of all faith, or none, in our pluralist, contemporary society. He does so from the particular context of hospital chaplaincy. He proposes that ecclesiology and missiology must always be grounded firmly in the person of Jesus Christ, especially on his example and teaching about non-sectarian human compassion. Chaplains find themselves on the cutting edge of ministry and mission – as they represent the Church (the body of Christ) while engaging with, and listening to, those who are outside the Church (but part of God's body in creation) in a 'secular' setting. From this perspective he notes the ways in which the Church deals with its internal diversity on the issues of parochial structure, liturgy and prayer, gender and sexuality and financial ethics in contrasting, and inconsistent, ways. In the light of this, he offers a vision of the Church as holy but also sick, as a way of ensuring that it is constantly called to self-critique and reform in the light of the Jesus whom we encounter in the Scriptures and the sacraments. Generosity, therefore, requires a robust sense of our own individual and corporate sinfulness and God's generous forgiveness, such that we are opened up to generative missiological collaboration partnership with others.

In considering ecclesiology and mission within Anglicanism, Jonathan Clark (Chapter 8) examines the nature of catholicity, rooted in the nature of God. This opens up a discussion about the nature of inclusivity. The inclusivity of the Church is to reflect the inclusivity of God, which presents particular challenges to the Christian community and to individuals. It demands that the story of the Bible is taken seriously; it means that tradition remains useful; it is something living and developing. A rich understanding of a generous loving God revealed in the Scriptures is given direction by our tradition, but it is the Spirit that guides us in the present and into the future. The Church must always be discerning because every place and time has different needs, or presents different opportunities. The purpose of the Church is not to ensure its own survival but that the world may know and respond to God's love. To fulfil that vocation, the Church needs to tell the same story, but differently.

Deepening Conversation in Generosity

Both *MSC* and *FTP* have shaped conversations about mission and ecclesiology. The former reminds us that the Church is to engage in creative and imaginative ways with our missionary calling. The latter affirms the place of inherited patterns and structures that cannot simply be discarded. The contributors of both publications affirm the importance of sacraments and the possibilities for mission. This book takes as its basis the uniqueness of the Church's calling in God's world, a world embraced by the generosity of his love. The Church is the body of Christ on the way: assured of salvation; committed to witnessing, listening and engaging; responsive and creative; faithful and critical. To live in relation to a generous God shapes our ecclesiology – all our ways of being, thinking, acting, praying and serving. This vocation is formed by a double constitution of worship and mission. This vocation is for the sake of the kingdom of God.

The various chapters in *Generous Ecclesiology* are offered as a contribution to an ongoing conversation. To this end, we engage with a rich range of dialogue partners, historically, ecumenically and culturally, as well as theologically. The book seeks to offer a rigorous theological resource – inspiring us to drink deeply of the wells of our tradition and inherited patterns. It also seeks to excite the Church about the possibilities for mission in our parishes, Fresh Expressions, chaplaincies and dioceses. Whether implicitly or explicitly, the chapters reflect on – or are shaped by – the ordinary concerns, challenges and opportunities of ministry. The particulars of tradition, locality, diocese or sector are held within a vision of the Church universal. The editors themselves have served as parish clergy in the London Diocese – as curates, associates vicars and incumbents. All of the contributors are actively involved in ministry – including preaching, pastoral care and sacramental worship. As such, this book is a precursor to a forthcoming set of essays on the practical outworking of a generous theology of the Church.

As partners of different traditions, churchmanship, and areas of ministry and life, there are inevitably differences in emphasis – and even disagreement – throughout this volume. This can be seen, for example, in different attitudes to 'incarnational theology', expressed in the chapters by Jeremy Morris, James Heard, Tom Greggs and in Ian Mobsby's Afterword. Part of what being generous means in this context is discussing, exploring and living with difference. It is this attitude to difference in the contexts of ecclesiology and mission that defines the overall vision that lies behind this project.

I

Generous Episcopacy

STEPHEN CONWAY

Introduction

The invitation to think about a generous and spacious episcopacy coincided with my engaging the diocese in which I had
recently arrived in a conversation that I have entitled *Imagining
the Future*.[1] For the conversation to be honest, the bishop has
to come clean that s/he arrives with prior formation and ideas
about the nature of God and the Church. I rejoice that the God
of mission chose a Church. It is not that the Church has a mission in its own right. I love the way light spills into a dark room
through an open door. I am drawn to a well-cared-for open
fire that heats the room and radiates light and steady warmth.
We are called to be lights of the One Light, Christ himself. We
radiate the light and warmth of Jesus, the true Fire of Love. We
are called to pulse with the light of the gospel – not as flares
so much as beams always emanating from the same constant
source. Some of the best paintings show light emerging from
inside the picture and not always coming from outside. We are
light radiating from the inside of God's canvas, which for us as
Anglicans is every parish, deanery and diocese *and* every other
part of the world with which we are linked. Fresh Expressions
of church, whether in ancient churches, modern buildings, in
the open air or on the internet, are also part of that canvas of
God. Bishops are called to serve transformation and order in
whatever landscape is painted. 'This includes the ability to send

---

1 Stephen Conway, *Imagining the Future: A Conversation Together*, Ely:
Diocesan Office, 2012.

fresh apostolic teams to cultures or areas where the mission presence is thin or non-existent.'[2]

The disciples on the road to Emmaus after the crucifixion told the stranger who had joined them on their journey what they had expected – which had not turned out as they had hoped. This could also be true of us: we had hoped that the Church would continue in its current shape, but this cannot be. That stranger on the Emmaus road with them, however, turned out to be the risen Christ, who instructed them in the Scriptures and showed them that it was not a time to remain in grief but to trust in the promise in Jesus' predictions of his passion: he would die, but be raised again on the third day. Being unprepared for the reality of the death, the disciples could not accept the certain promise of new life. It is deep in our DNA as Christians that we only enjoy Easter Day because we have come to the cross on Good Friday. We are Easter People through being Calvary's Children.

'Imagining' in a study of ecclesiology fits well with the encounter along the road to Emmaus. A risky but gracious future becomes possible because the risen Lord personally rehearses the truth of the Scriptures with them and reveals himself in the sacramental act of breaking bread. Christ reminded the sad and fainthearted of the sovereignty and faithfulness of the God who has a good purpose for the universe. The New Creation has begun in the resurrection of Jesus, who so breathed upon the apostles that they ran rejoicing back into the places of risk and danced in the Way.

Defenders of Faith and Focus of Unity

Bishops are called to be the right defenders of the faith received from those apostles, whose authority they bear. The apostolic succession is not a magic or mechanical transmission of privilege and power from the apostles until today: it is the continuity of apostolic faith and faithfulness in mission and

---

2 *MSC*, p. 136.

ministry signified by the continuity of the laying on of hands by bishops upon those coming after them. *The Porvoo Common Statement* elucidates this:

> To ordain a bishop in the historic succession ... is also a sign. In so doing the Church communicates its care for continuity in the whole of its life and mission, and reinforces its determination to manifest the permanent characteristics of the Church of the Apostles.[3]

Bishops are spoken of as those who defend the deposit of the faith, but this must not be represented as a static phenomenon. At every licensing and institution, the officiating bishop reads the *Declaration of Assent* before the oaths are sworn.[4] This makes plain that the faith once given by the apostles has to be interpreted faithfully in and to every generation. The tradition is a large room into which people need to be invited to draw on the richness. They need the tools so that they are neither frozen to the spot nor frantically rushing and not settling. A bishop exasperated his wife because he kept giving people help with the clues on a treasure hunt, because he saw it as his episcopal calling to do so. This definitely does not mean that we fritter away our inheritance, however. *FTP* is right to stand against a devaluing into values of the marks of the Church and to advocate the guarantee of them in the Canons of the Church of England.[5]

Prophets to Church Culture

The bishop has a prophetic calling too. Many of the prophets among the Hebrews had nothing to do with the Temple and

---

3 Council for Christian Unity of the General Synod of the Church of England, *The Porvoo Common Statement*, London: Church House Publishing, 1993, p. 27.

4 Archbishops' Council, *Common Worship: Services and Prayers for the Church of England*, London: Church House Publishing, 2000, p. xi. See also Colin Podmore, *Aspects of Anglican Identity*, London: Church House Publishing, 2005, pp. 43–57.

5 *FTP*, p. 74.

the religious establishment. Priests and the cult in general were their targets. First Isaiah was obviously close to the royal court, however, as was Nathan under David. Jeremiah was not from Jerusalem, but came to live close to the heart of the cult in Jerusalem. Ezekiel was a priest as well as a prophet. Bishops have to live with the tension of being both at the heart of 'the Temple' and yet not bound to it. The language Ezekiel uses as a prophet is rather distinct from that of others with a prophetic calling, but that is because he is a priest as well. He stepped beyond the bounds of the priesthood in his proclamation that the glory of God was no longer restricted to the Temple in Jerusalem, but had travelled to be with the exiles in Babylon. At the same time, the second half of his prophecy is closely concerned with the detailed provisions of the heavenly temple of the future. A bishop is bound to remember that Christ promised to rebuild the Temple in three days in his body. Jeremiah 7 is often interpreted as the prophet's writing off of the efficacy of the worship of the Temple. This is really a lament because it was not taken seriously enough. The bishop is not giving up on the Church, but looking to see where the glory of God has come to rest so that all can manifest church there with the most wonderful worship that can be mustered.

Bishops have their seats in cathedrals and minster churches which, in this generation, are experiencing a revival. Cathedrals look like they bear every weight of the tradition and the Church's history and are described as the mother churches of their dioceses, because they house the bishop's cathedra or seat of authority. In practice, however, the experience of cathedrals in England anyway is that they are often at the edge of the Church, spending most of their time setting out the Christian faith to visitors who have little to do with traditional church life. The goal of the cathedral is to turn visitors into pilgrims. Similarly, bishops who are so much at the centre of church life need properly to remain agnostic about a good deal of it – not to make the Church or themselves the butt of mockery, but to have a measure of prophetic humour about it. The perspective is that we have been given 2,000 years of gospel life so far, but it is all built on three years, even three days. Bishops as leaders in mission do not stand still guarding the treasures, but lead the people out, expecting God's treasures yet to be revealed.[6]

Bishops need, therefore, to be those whose primary concern is the culture of a diocese rather than its particular strategies and policies. Clergy often and properly complain about initiative fatigue. This complaint is sometimes a symptom of the fact that policies are at odds with the implicit or explicit culture and mood of a diocese. Culture eats strategy for breakfast. Unless the bishop is passionate about the desired mission culture in all its forms and believes in making new disciples, why should anyone else be excited and energized? We have a false dichotomy between traditional parochial ministry and the development of Fresh Expressions of church. Some cry that we should get 'old church' right before we deliver 'liquid and café church'. We forget, however, that the roots of the parish system in the ministries of early medieval reformers like St Dunstan were precisely in a passion for evangelism within a settled rhythm of worship and service. Bishops are called to a pattern of transforming leadership that seeks to model a culture that sustains all the marks of the Church proclaimed in our creeds, and that does so in as many sustainable settings as possible. It also follows that Fresh Expressions of church are not excused from living within this culture.[7]

Although they are mentioned in passing, in a sentence in the theological chapter, *MSC* would have benefited from a wider consideration of 'The Five Marks of Mission':

To proclaim the Good News of the Kingdom
To teach, baptize and nurture new believers
To respond to human need by loving service
To seek to transform unjust structures of society
To strive to safeguard the integrity of creation and sustain and renew the life of the earth.[8]

---

6 Theos and The Grubb Institute, *Spiritual Capital: The Present and Future of English Cathedrals*, London: Theos, 2012, see especially chapter 5, pp. 55ff.

7 *MSC*, pp. 96–100.

8 Developed by the Anglican Consultative Council between 1984 and 1990 and adopted by the Church of England in 1996. See the Anglican Communion

Salisbury and Ely are two among the dioceses that have sought to grow a culture built around The Five Marks. The Church of England's recent report *World-Shaped Mission* gives us a clear picture of the claims of integral mission.[9] We have created an easily remembered set of five 't's: *tell, teach, tend, transform* and *treasure*. I shall now be stretched to come up with a sixth 't' to express the Church's decision to add reconciliation to the list. The experience of living The Five Marks so far is that no parish or other community lives out all five equally at any one time or, perhaps, ever. None the less, we want to avoid any parish or Fresh Expression believing that it is let off the hook of genuine concern for integral mission. Not all of us will raise up pioneer ministers, either. The point is that we should be encouraging a pioneering culture in which all of us are adventurous. Western theology is not just the doctrine of the Western Church rooted in Augustine; it could be a theology inspired by the experience of missionary Christians in the westward expansion of the United States who understood that the pioneer and the settler may be one and the same person.[10]

Refreshed Expressions of Bishop

Many Fresh Expressions are refreshed expressions attempted differently and with fresh energy in a new situation. Rather than entirely Fresh Expressions of a bishop, refreshed models of episcopacy from our tradition might be illuminating. Our traditional monarchical model of episcopacy is derived from the letters of St Ignatius, the first-century Bishop of Antioch, to young church communities (Ephesians, Magnesians, Trallians, Romans, Philadelphians and Smyrnaeans) and to Polycarp, Bishop of Smyrna, and was refined in the Middle Ages.[11] It has

website for further information: www.anglicancommunion.org/ministry/mission/fivemarks.cfm (accessed 27 November 2012).

9 Janice Price, *World-Shaped Mission: Reimagining Mission Today*, London: Church House Publishing, 2012.

10 Wes Seelinger, *Western Theology*, Cordova, TN: Spring Arbor Distributors, 1985.

11 J. H. Srawley (ed.), *The Epistles of St Ignatius, Bishop of Antioch*, London: SPCK, 1935.

been held in check in practice in our English setting by episcopal absenteeism about national business until the late nineteenth century, combined with the effect of a much smaller episcopate. It is a powerful model that ironically has been strengthened in the popular imagination by the creation of synodical government and its House of Bishops. This model is having a considerable impact upon our debate about the authority of bishops and provision for opponents of women in the episcopate. Bishops have the apostolic authority to do what Ignatius says, which is to represent Christ. The question is about how that representation is exercised. An even earlier model in the early Church is that of Clement of Rome, who appears to have operated a much more conciliar pattern. This gained some renewed interest during the debates at the Restoration about the nature of episcopacy. Edward Reynolds, who became Bishop of Norwich (1660–76), advocated a kind of 'reduced episcopacy' very much on the Clementine model. Reynolds had begun to see on theological grounds that unity and moderation were served by applying the best of Presbyterianism to reformed episcopacy to create at least a modicum of collaborative leadership.[12]

MSC quotes the Chicago–Lambeth Quadrilateral, declared by the General Convention of the Protestant Episcopal Church in 1886 and adopted by the Lambeth Conference in 1888, when it states that 'The historic episcopate is locally adapted in the methods of its administration to the varying needs of the nations and peoples called of God into the unity of his Church.'[13] Bishop Charles Gore wrote in The Church and the Ministry that the ministry of bishops is directly derived from

---

12 Oxford Dictionary of National Biography, online edition: www.oxford dnb.com/view/article/23408?docPos=2 (accessed 27 November 2012).

13 The Chicago–Lambeth Quadrilateral enshrines four points of agreement: the Holy Scriptures of the Old and New Testaments as the revealed word of God; the Nicene Creed as the sufficient statement of the Christian faith; the two sacraments – Baptism and the Supper of the Lord – ministered with unfailing use of Christ's words of institution and of the elements ordained by him; the historic episcopate, locally adapted in the methods of its administration to the varying needs of the nations and peoples called of God into the unity of his Church. See the Anglican Communion website: www.anglicancommunion.org/resources/ acis/docs/chicago_lambeth_quadrilateral.cfm (accessed 27 November 2012).

the apostles.[14] He was clear in other writings, however, that the local church had great freedom to organize itself and set its own tone.[15] We read in Bede's *Ecclesiastical History* of what is perhaps the most attractive model we inherit in Britain, the Celtic model of Saints Aidan and Cuthbert.[16] Melrose is an attractive town in the Scottish Borders where St Aidan planted the first successful Irish monastic mission from the island of Iona in what was then the Kingdom of Northumbria. The essential unit of the local church was the monastery, which was very commonly led by a lay abbot. Bishops were accorded all the authority of their office, but they were not expected to run the organization. That is why it was not strange at all for Cuthbert to be able to retire to Lindisfarne for sustained periods while he was an active bishop and why the Church did not fail when he went into complete retreat on the Inner Farne. The bishop's job was literally, as well as figuratively, to go and plant the cross, proclaim the gospel, and offer the sacraments and to be indifferent as to whether that was in the hall of the king or – as more commonly in the case both of Aidan and Cuthbert – in the high valleys where the poor and unremarked lived, after the pattern of Christ's seeking the lost and those on the margins. My own experience tells me that this drenching in local mission brings the bishop back to essentials. Moreover, it is so important for the culture, as an expression of leadership that is rooted in various definitions of what 'local' can mean. Long before *MSC* was advocating the same thing, *Episcopal Ministry*, the Report of the Archbishops' Group on the Episcopate, asserts very clearly that pressures of administration and other demands on the bishop are in conflict with the bishop's primary role in mission.[17] The model of the bishop who is free

14 Charles Gore, *The Church and the Ministry*, London and Oxford: Rivingtons, 1919 [1886].

15 Charles Gore, *The Basis of Anglican Fellowship in Faith and Organization: An Open Letter to the Clergy of the Diocese of Oxford*, London: Mowbray, 1909; reprinted 1914.

16 Judith McClure and Roger Collins (eds), *Bede's Ecclesiastical History of the English People*, Oxford: Oxford World's Classics, 1999.

17 Archbishops' Group on the Episcopate, *Episcopal Ministry*, London: Church House Publishing, 1994.

enough from busy-ness to be planting the cross regularly in communities across the diocese is powerful and attractive.

Leadership, Distributed Authority and Discipline

Good leadership is an essential characteristic of the bishop in mission. As part of that leadership, the bishop needs to ensure that there is good management of the Church's human and financial resources. The primary duty of the bishop is to take responsibility for how the local church inculturates the gospel and the marks of the Church. This includes taking the lead in being purposeful, rigorous and transparent with regard to money and management, and anything else. The bishop ensures this, but should not have to deliver it. The pivotal verse in Luke is 9.53, when Jesus turns his face towards Jerusalem. It still takes a lot of travelling and teaching before he gets there. There is no doubting the direction and purpose of Jesus, but I wonder how much he was involved in planning the daily itinerary as he and the disciples criss-crossed Galilee and the Decapolis? I have been on the boats from Seahouses to the Farne Islands many times. Cuthbert's retreat will have felt like a watery desert perfect for the ascetic, but it was mostly reachable for those seeking guidance from the bishop about the direction of the mission of the Church. I used the word 'spacious' in the introduction as a qualification of 'generous' advisedly. Cuthbert offered spacious leadership by drawing in the poor who were otherwise excluded. He also took the non-neurotic choice of the leader to create space for leadership – much of which he had inspired – by withdrawing from the space himself. Decisively, he prayed and kept in touch when he was on the Inner Farne. At other times, he located his leadership in the midst, drilling down to the depths where the life is. Not surprisingly, he was mirroring the life of God. The Father exercised perfect humility in withdrawing himself so that there was room for creation to happen. The Son laid aside his glory to be the servant of all in his incarnation.

In the light of the above, there is a lively experiment currently in the Diocese of Ely to work with episcopal authority that is distributed and shared, but not abdicated. This presents a primary characteristic of episcopal leadership: it is the fount of distributed authority, which enables and encourages all Christians to exercise the leadership gifts that emerge from their formation as disciples, and as they take their full place in the ordering of God's Church. This means that authority is given away to the extent that people are expected to take responsibility for the roles and tasks assigned to them so that if they make mistakes, they can grow through them to fresh insight and reflective action. This does not mean that I distance myself from the person or the risk; rather, it means that I actively seek to enable individuals and groups to take effective responsibility for shared leadership, when delegation is more likely to enable the transformation of any situation. This commitment to collaborative leadership is an expectation upon all those called to exercise leadership throughout the Diocese of Ely, whether ordained or lay. The common purpose in mission leads us into shared ministry in our communities so that individual ministries emerge out of, and are nurtured by, teams of people working together, both lay and ordained. Under the bishop, every community will have its acknowledged leader. Just as the bishop distributes his authority to many people without abdicating it, so shared leadership in local communities can be vital and liberating without losing a sense of the location of responsibility.

I was careful to say that every community will have an acknowledged leader, not that that person will necessarily be ordained. A contemporary iteration of the Celtic model might appropriately suggest that the leader in mission might be a volunteer lay person and that the stipendiary priest is the accompanier of that leader and that community. The priest would not abdicate a profound teaching and spiritual leadership, but she would not in those circumstances direct the community. This is not a model to defend lazy or fearful priests. It might be a way, however, to encourage renewed thinking about a mixed economy of ministry as well as of mission. This may also be a way to a richer understanding of the place of active retired clergy and those who offer house for duty ministry. I have had good experience in two dioceses of the impact of intentional interim ministry. I have seen this work effectively at both parish and episcopal level in the Episcopal Church in the United States where vacancies are even longer than ours in the Church of England. Bishops are commonly upbraided by church wardens for not getting on with filling their vacancy. Just occasionally they repent and thank bishops for giving them the space in which to grow. The work of archdeacons and rural deans as accompanying priests is vital as an extension of episcopal accompaniment. Of course, it fits with the Clementine model of collegial episcopacy. It fits even better with the walking alongside model of Aidan and Cuthbert. Aidan kept refusing King Oswald's offer of a horse because he refused to travel above the heads of the poor, but only side by side with them. Modern parents do not eschew horsepower, but invite their teenage children to come out for a ride in the car because they will have a much more adult conversation side by side than in distant confrontation. This applies equally in ecclesial communities.

Notwithstanding this, there are times when the bishop has to exercise determining authority, mostly in seeking to transform conflicts and establish fairness and mutual accountability. This applies in the area of Fresh Expressions. The bishop is often the defender of experiments in ministry and evangelism and must be the protector and promoter of those who strive and sometimes fail. The bishop should be presenting Jim or Joan as glorious examples of responsible risk-taking for God. The bishop is also the guardian of right intention when the ordering of things may not be linear. With a Fresh Expression living out my instruction to be sacramental from the start, I remain ignorant of the exact interaction of baptism and Eucharist. Paradoxically, the bishop exercises a firm authority over the ordering of the Church precisely so that there can be a readiness for 'Messy Diocese' to break out. On the other hand, the bishop must protect parishes and deaneries from uncontrolled planting that does not have the active consent of the wider Church. There is a limit even to the authority of bishops if groups go ahead anyway. The bishop does not determine whether or not a community is preaching the gospel or living a sacrificial Christian life. However, as Hooker understood, the office of bishop has proven to be the best focus for the unity and leadership of the Church with scriptural warrant that has so far been invented. It is therefore for the bishop to decide whom to license and recognize as belonging fully within the ecclesial bounds of the Church of England within the wider orbit of the whole Church. *MSC* alludes accurately to the particular brokering role of the bishop.

Missionary Territory and Partnership

It is not accidental that I am reflecting upon ancient models of episcopal ministry, most of which pre-date our parish system. Until parishes became very clearly defined not only as worshipping communities but as pieces of property, the diocese was evidently the base unit of the Church and remains so in catholic ecclesiology as expressed in the role of the bishop, through the exercise of discipline and in the nurture, formation and the provision of clergy. We often ardently proclaim that the parochial system is the foundation of the Church of England. None the less, there were bishops and dioceses long before there were parishes. This is not an expression of episcopal chutzpah. Rather, it is an invitation to reconsider what 'local' means in our church and in society as we experience it. Like many of the Church's ministers, much of the bishop's ministry is properly ministry across and within the whole community. Especially as Anglicans, we believe passionately that all human geography is important. The *parochia* of the bishop is the whole area, the name of which he has taken as his/her identity. When the bishop shares the cure of souls with other deacons and priests, s/he is sharing that identity with place and people with them. We would often choose to think that 'local' is shorthand for settled community, but in reality often it is not. We live in a society that is being thoroughly suburbanized in the sense that increasing numbers of people do not live where they sleep. Their sense of belonging is elsewhere, including spiritually.

This creates the challenge that we have institutional chaplains in health and education and other sectors who are treated as the 'vicar' of the whole community, while parish clergy are under huge pressure to retreat into chaplaincy to the people who pay for them. The authors of *FTP* see episcopacy undermined by management groups for Fresh Expressions, which draw in support and action from people who are not local and even from outside the diocese.[18] In some way this is seen to compromise the authority of the bishop. The point is that such groups are set up with the bishop's approval, especially where Bishops' Mission Orders apply. A bishop has no such influence over individual or corporate patrons, or the ordering of the Christian life of Oxbridge colleges.

As the exemplary tone and pacesetter for a generous ecclesial culture, the bishop has to be as flexible as possible with the structures that s/he oversees for the sake of both emerged and emerging patterns of mission and ministry. I have rich experience of the vital place of schools and colleges in the Church's mission. Many schools are already or emerging ecclesial communities in which the clergy have access to cross-generational communities at the heart of parishes and benefices in which discipling may be happening more obviously than in the parish church. It is for the bishop to defend the clergy for spending time with people who may come to active faith, but never darken the door of the parish church on a Sunday morning. This is the bugbear at the heart of the debate between Fresh Expressions and settled church: old church pays for all this but may not see the benefits in its own terms. We could construe 'local' in another way, however, and see that we might all feel more engaged in a common enterprise if we rejoiced to see a number of ways of being church across a deanery. *MSC* properly refers to the strategic role of deaneries.[19] The first of my predecessors who lived fully in the Diocese of Ely, Bishop Harold Browne, was a great proponent of the deanery when the model began to take shape after the middle of the nine-

---

18 *FTP*, p. 73.
19 *MSC*, p. 136.

teenth century.[20] We have tended to see the deanery in mostly financial and bureaucratic terms as the body that works out the distribution of the parish share. The deaneries hold great promise as the principal mission areas of any diocese. Rural deans are among the bishop's key colleagues in promoting and serving the mission of God and should be cherished as they share directly in *episcope*. The deanery has both the scope and the locality to nurture and hold to account new and established styles of pastoral ministry, evangelism and social action. Team ministries can work well, but risk becoming so bound up in their own structures that all their energy is consumed keeping the team running. Spacious deaneries have the capacity to be quite playful with opportunities within an existing structure that models representative and licensed authority. We need a particular drive to encourage the real leaders of communities to come forward to serve the deanery as their primary calling. A ground-breaking conversation took place in a meeting of a large rural team during a vacancy when, after a few voices spoke up loudly on behalf of an intensely local view of community and ministry, others quietly pointed out that many others only stayed with the very local because they had access to the life of the whole team. A mixed economy approach to ministry might open up opportunities for some priests to be very local, but for the majority of full-time clergy to be deployed across the whole territory of deanery or team. It all still assumes the encouragement of the bishop, who already models belonging to every church and to all churches in the diocese.

Holy Order and All God's Companions

Criticisms of the movement for Fresh Expressions and church-planting express a profound agnosticism about what can be seen as anxious attempts to scramble into a postmodern landscape. There is a rush to defend what is too precious to lose in what could degenerate from a 'mixed economy' to a 'free

20 Frances Knight, 'Bishops of Ely 1864–1957', in Peter Meadows (ed.), *Ely: Bishops and Diocese 1109–2009*, Woodbridge: Boydell Press, 2010, pp. 259–86.

market' in which the treasures of our reformed catholic traditions could be traded away for the sake of a false relevance.
MSC is at pains to place itself at the heart of the living stream
of Anglican ecclesiology. The planting of new churches and
carving out new mission areas has been a constant theme of
the Church's mission. Present experimentation does not change
that; nor does it fundamentally undermine the parochial system.
This is partly a matter of scale and capacity, but also largely
because of the continuing resilience of the parochial model and
what it says about our calling to the whole turf of our country. One does not need to contrive an argument with the Fresh
Expressions movement, however, to be concerned about our
wholehearted celebration of order and sacramentality. This
is not an argument with MSC. It is a profound disagreement
with those who would argue that our huge rejoicing over lay
ministries means that we celebrate the fullness of holy order
less. I proclaim in the Diocese of Ely that I have such a high
view of holy order that I have no anxiety about the flourishing
of lay ministry and discipleship. Many of us also take a seriously different view about the genuine counter-cultural basis
for Fresh Expressions. Of course there has to be flexibility, as I
have already argued. None the less, Fresh Expressions must intend to express all the marks of the Church as soon as possible.
There is a powerful theological fallacy that priests and sacraments are almost embarrassments in the development of Fresh
Expressions. This is based on an assumption and an experience
of order and sacraments as restrictions, and not freedoms in
which all should share. Relying on them is not the issue for
mission; only how they are imagined and celebrated.

The purpose of holy order is to reflect and live out in and for
the world the wonderful economy of God. We are all as much
involved as each other. Tertullian described confirmation as
the ordination of the laity. We are all called to be witnesses
of Christ's saving love, and the greatest part of that witness
is offered by lay people. The most renowned theologians of
the Church are engaged in the same enterprise as the humble
teacher of Sunday School or After School Club. The calling of
Christian teachers is a calling to participate in the formation of

every Christian, shared with those preparing people for ordination and other public ministries. John 15 reminds us at the
same time that we are called to be the fruitful friends of Jesus
and that this calling, too, is shared. Paul refers to himself and
Apollos as *synergoi* or 'fellow-workers' (1 Corinthians 3.9)
and Prisca is given the same title in Romans 16.3.

All bishops are priests and represent the fullness of that
priesthood for the Church and with their fellow presbyters. All
clergy, whether serving parishes or other kinds of community,
have authority derived from their ordination; but they are all
licensed to serve particular ministries with a cure of souls that
the bishop shares with them. The deacon leads people by the
hand and by example in and through their real-life context to
the point at which transformation becomes a real possibility.
The servant of that transformation is the priest who lives out a
calling that is shaped by the work of the Redemption wrought
for all through the suffering, death and resurrection of Christ.
The bishop and all priests offer the sacraments that transform
the ordinary, so that water brings new life through baptism,
bread and wine become for us the body and blood of Christ,
and the fruit of sunshine and the earth produces the oil of healing and gladness. This sacramental transformation is meant
also to happen to the walking talking sacraments who are the
human beings who have been welcomed into Christ's life and
who have welcomed him into theirs.

The bishop, like all priests, lives keenly the imagery and hope
of Romans 8, encouraging people in their groaning, in their
waiting for the completion of all things in Christ. Using the
model of spiritual direction, the bishop must be attentive – and
even respectful – towards the current context and outlook of
the person, but spiritual direction is not the equivalent of non-
directive counselling: it has a clear purpose in pointing people
beyond where they are to the new place where God is coming
to meet them. This is what formation means. Like the angel, the
priest is directing people to Galilee, to the place of resurrection
encounter. This does not mean a leapfrogging from Palm Sunday to Easter Day, missing out Good Friday. The priest seeks to
draw individuals and communities of grace to live at the heart

of new creation, to know what it means to have our heart of stone replaced by a heart of flesh. That heart of flesh, moreover, is the sacred heart of Christ. The priest leads the community in proclaiming the victory from the vantage point of a bloody tree outside the gate on which the Son of God has died.

The bishop proclaims that he died that we, too, might die to sin and live to God in Jesus Christ. Identifying with people in their situation is absolutely necessary and many of us have come a cropper by thinking that we had the remedy for their situation before we got there. Trusting in God going ahead of us and being already present with individuals and communities, the interaction of the diaconal and priestly roles, finds the point at which the challenge to move on can be offered out of the language and experience of that person or community. Identifying with the poor does not mean that the poor are always right. The bishop needs huge reserves of compassionate patience for others and for herself/himself as space and time for growth are provided and prayed in. As the servant of transformation, the bishop with all his/her priests ministers in 'the now-and-not-yet' in the way that Paul and John have elaborated. For John, the cross is the throne of victory but the fulfilment is yet to come. In responding to the churches that he founded, Paul is constantly challenged by the desire to hold all the urgency of the imminence of Christ's return and the growing acceptance that we actually need to live with Christ's immanence, his clear presence in the Spirit through many generations.

Decisive to this service of transformation offered by the bishop and other priests and ministers is the priestly role as missionary teacher, introducing people fresh to the life of God through the teaching of God's word in Holy Scripture, and giving existing disciples the tools to interpret the world and God's action within it. The bishops' authority to ordain and commission can be interpreted as an expression of the missionary emphasis of their ministry exemplified in their own practice. New Testament definitions of apostleship put the stress less on the inherent authority of the person or office than upon the purity of witness to the crucified and risen Christ. Therefore, the bishop and his/her priests have to be able to point to the saving work of Christ in their own lives. So s/he should be a skilled teacher whose life is marked by the character of Christ. As an evangelist, the bishop can be described as one who brings new Christians to birth. This is still expressed symbolically in the primary role of the bishop in the initiation of new Christians at baptism and the sealing of the call of the adult believer through confirmation.

The foundation of the call of anyone to be a bishop is God's earnest demand that we all turn to Christ to get a life as adventurous disciples. Everything is rooted in our growing into the character of Christ, being cross-shaped people who have a joyful and playful trust in the risen life of Christ. Now is the time to reclaim the rich fullness of our faith by putting down deeper roots in prayer, study and celebration so that we can all hear the call of the Christ who comes to us, stays with us and sends us. Wherever Jesus went he gathered friends around him. He still does. We claim companionship with God because God no longer calls us servants but friends. To be God's friend is our highest ambition, but it can feel like our greatest failure. We need to rely profoundly on the Holy Spirit praying in us. Friends need to keep in touch. Jesus is always moving towards us, leaping over all the barriers we erect to keep him at bay. We need to include penitence too. We need to be stripped for action by our sorrow for sin and our readiness to accept the forgiveness of Christ. He longs to forgive us so that we can step up to the mark as adventurous disciples. We cannot reach the bar ourselves, but Jesus is all the lift we need. We should desire a character of friendship that makes us friends and companions with one another, which reveals our companionship with God. Our ministry should express not just a sense of community that is human, but the bonds of communion that is divine, the pure gift of sharing the life of the Trinity. Communion is God's gift, but we are the ones who can break it. I am always thrilled when I meet people who are living translations of the gospel. If we seek the real presence of Christ not only in the Eucharist but also in the Word proclaimed and lived, then we shall bear fruit as real companions for whom bread becomes the life of God to us.

2

Building Community: Anglo-Catholicism and Social Action

JEREMY MORRIS

Introduction

Some years ago the *Guardian* reporter Stuart Jeffries spent a day with a Salvation Army couple on the Meadows estate in Nottingham. When he asked them why they had gone there, he got what to him was obviously a baffling reply: 'It's called incarnational living. It's from John chapter 1. You know that bit about "Jesus came among us." It's all about living in the community rather than descending on it to preach.'[1] It is telling that the phrase 'incarnational living' had to be explained, but there is all the same something a little disconcerting in hearing from the mouth of a Salvation Army officer an argument that you would normally expect to hear from the catholic wing of Anglicanism. William Booth would surely have been a little disconcerted by that rider 'rather than descending on it to preach', because the early history and missiology of the Salvation Army, in its marching into working-class areas and its street preaching, was *precisely* about cultural invasion, expressed in language of challenge, purification, conversion and 'saving souls', and not characteristically in the language of incarnationalism. Yet it goes to show that the Salvation Army has not been immune to the broader history of Christian theology in this country, and that it too has been influenced by

---

1 *Guardian*, 'With God's Army', 17 December 2008.

that current of ideas that first emerged clearly in the middle of the nineteenth century, and that has come to be called the Anglican tradition of social witness.

My aim in this chapter is to say something of the beginnings of this movement and of its continuing relevance today, by offering a historical redescription of its origins, attending particularly to some of its earliest and most influential advocates, including the theologians F. D. Maurice (1805–72) and Charles Gore (1853–1932). Maurice was certainly a theologian of the incarnation in that classic mid- and late-nineteenth-century sense, and the slightly later Gore was probably the best known of all of those who followed on more or less from the inspiration of Maurice's social theology. Gore, in the eyes of many, effectively fused Maurice's Christian Socialism on to High Church Anglicanism and created what became a highly influential school of Anglo-Catholic social radicalism. Yet it would be a mistake to pin everything on just one or two seminal figures, for my argument here is above all that this was, and is, a profoundly inventive *tradition*, which encompassed or drew on various influences and which cannot be pigeonholed in the reactionary, ritual-obsessed way that some of its fiercest opponents have assumed. It cannot be traced back only to Maurice, for many of its liveliest concerns had quite a different source, and were central to those very Oxford Movement leaders from whom Maurice himself broke away. What emerges from my attempt to 're-read' this tradition is a picture of a positive and creative attention to the building of Christian community, in a way that avoided the mere repetition of existing pastoral strategies, and that was genuinely experimental, while being no less traditional for all that. The theological inspiration of this tradition unquestionably lay in the heavy accent that High Church Anglicans came to place on the doctrine of the incarnation, but they pursued an integrated vision of faith in which community action, liturgy, personal devotion, education and theology cohered in a sacramental and incarnational way of viewing the world, and not least in the Eucharist.

A re-reading of this tradition is necessary today, not only because of its relative neglect among those who read Christian theology, but because the particular movement of Christian Socialism with which Maurice's name, and those of others, is also associated has itself been almost written out of the conventional histories of the British Left. Admittedly Christian Socialism is a subset of the broader tradition of Anglican social theology, but it is an especially significant subset and one that is central to the view many Anglicans continue to hold of their influence on the evolution of British social policy. Yet outside the Anglican world, this influence is commonly disputed or ignored. Yes, we like to *say* things like the Labour movement owed more to Methodism than to Marx, but that is not generally how Labour historians have seen things. Much more prominent in the historiography of the Left has been the view put forward by one of the early propagandists of the quasi-Marxist Social Democratic Federation, a forerunner of the Labour Party, who claimed that 'it is as reasonable to speak of Christian Socialism as it would be to speak of Christian Arithmetic or Christian Geometry'.[2] Marx himself had written in the *Communist Manifesto* that 'Christian Socialism is but the holy water with which the priest consecrates the heart-burnings of the aristocrat'.[3] Another early socialist apologist, Ernest Belfort Bax, dismissed the Guild of St Matthew, a radical Anglican organization formed by Stewart Headlam (1847–1924), a disciple of F. D. Maurice, as 'merely [representing] a phase common to ages of transition in which the reactionary ideal and morality endeavours to steal a march on the progressive ideal and morality'.[4]

It is hardly surprising that that view has never been very attractive in Anglican circles. Here instead there has been almost the opposite tendency, the creation of a mythology – fed by the example of the great slum-priests – of Anglo-Catholic

---

2 James Leathem, quoted in G. Johnson, 'British Social Democracy and Religion, 1881–1911', *Journal of Ecclesiastical History*, vol. 51.1 (2000), p. 108. Johnson's article presents a much more mixed and nuanced picture than this quotation itself suggests.

3 Karl Marx, *The Revolutions of 1848*, ed. D. Fernbach, Harmondsworth: Penguin, 1973, p. 89. Marx had France in mind, and not Britain, since the British Christian Socialist movement had not got off the ground when he wrote this.

4 Quoted in Johnson, 'British Social Democracy and Religion', p. 108.

identification with the poor that could even promote Anglo-Catholicism as the Anglican equivalent of liberation theology.[5] The long history of Anglican social witness that stems from Maurice, Gore and others is often assumed to have found its practical expression in the slum-priests of the late nineteenth and early twentieth centuries, men such as Robert Dolling of Portsmouth and the East End, who supposedly said of his own social commitments that 'I speak out and fight about the drains because I believe in the Incarnation'.[6] The mythology of the slum-priest cries out for a certain debunking, and yet also a certain re-mythologizing. Debunking, because, however seriously one takes the social commitment of those outstanding characters, the 'slum-priests' were not unique, but simply one further instance of the extraordinary reach of the British churches into the heart of the cities in the nineteenth century. There were plenty of evangelical parallels – not only remarkably committed and able evangelical Anglicans, but a host of nonconformist or pan-evangelical bodies such as the London City Mission; the Christian Mission and then its successor the Salvation Army; the Primitive Methodists; the Methodist Central Missions of the late nineteenth century; the ragged schools; and so on.[7] We have to re-read all these initiatives in concert with a re-reading of the history of religion in Britain, dispensing with much that has passed for common knowledge about the assumed (but

5 This is not quite the same point as that made by John Vincent about the possibility of a modern British liberation theology, for which see C. Rowland's introduction to the *Cambridge Companion to Liberation Theology*, Cambridge: Cambridge University Press, 1999, pp. 14–15, though Vincent does draw on some historical precedents.

6 C. E. Osborne, *The Life of Father Dolling*, 3rd edn, London: Arnold, 1903, p. 245. Actually, Osborne does not put this quote directly in the mouth of Dolling, though other sources – for example, a pamphlet published by the Catholic Literature Association in 1933 and available online at www.anglicanhistory.org/bios/rwrdolling.html (accessed 5 January 2009) – seem to have assumed he did.

7 See, for example, K. Heasman, *Evangelicals in Action*, London: Bles, 1962; K. S. Inglis, *Churches and the Working Classes in Victorian England*, London: Routledge & Kegan Paul, 1963; J. Wolffe (ed.), *Evangelical Faith and Public Zeal: Evangelicals and Society in Britain, 1780–1980*, London: SPCK, 1995; F. K. Prochaska, *Christianity and Social Service in Modern Britain: The Disinherited Spirit*, Oxford: Oxford University Press, 2006.

illusory) history of secularization.[8] What emerges is not so much the picture of a few heroic individuals, as of a heroic religious *culture*. And I say that, even without taking anything away from the evident indifference and suspicion with which the work of religious professionals was popularly regarded in the Victorian and Edwardian era, and for which there is a lot of compelling evidence.[9]

And then *re*-mythologizing. What Anglo-Catholicism, and the Anglican social tradition more broadly, helped to create was nevertheless a movement with a distinct theological character, and genuine social commitment. Maurice – who was not himself classifiable as an Anglo-Catholic, though arguably he was a High Churchman – did outline a theological method that helped many Anglicans to move beyond the economic individualism which sat comfortably beside the preoccupation of evangelicals and early High Churchmen alike with personal redemption and sin.[10] What he and others signalled was captured a little too neatly by the historian Boyd Hilton, in his claim that around the middle of the nineteenth century British theology moved out of an 'age of atonement' and into an 'age of incarnation'.[11] Maurice was not alone among Anglican theologians in his scepticism of political economy, the 'dismal science' of Carlyle's famous diatribe.[12] Again contrary to the well-worn prejudices of some, it is clear (as I shall show) that even the

---

8 Cf. D. H. McLeod, *Secularisation in Western Europe, 1848–1914*, Basingstoke: Macmillan, 2000, and also the more extreme statement of C. G. Brown, *The Death of Christian Britain: Understanding Secularisation, 1800–2000*, London: Routledge, 2000. For a critical review of the latter, see J. Morris, 'The Strange Death of Christian Britain: Another Look at the Secularization Debate', *Historical Journal*, vol. 46.4 (2003), pp. 963–76.

9 One of the best discussions of this is S. C. Williams, *Religious Belief and Popular Culture in Southwark, c.1880–1939*, Oxford: Oxford University Press, 1999.

10 On this, see especially A. M. C. Waterman, *Revolution, Economics and Religion: Christian Political Economy, 1798–1833*, Cambridge: Cambridge University Press, 1991.

11 B. Hilton, *The Age of Atonement: The Influence of Evangelicalism on Social and Economic Thought, 1795–1865*, Oxford: Oxford University Press, 1988.

12 T. Carlyle, 'Occasional Discourse on the Nigger Question', in I. Campbell (ed.), *Thomas Carlyle: Selected Essays*, new edn, London: Dent, 1915, p. 308.

early Tractarians themselves were profoundly concerned about the well-being of society as a whole, and committed to a vision of the Church as a great engine of social reform.

What all this suggests is that the Anglican tradition of social criticism still has a lot going for it, for it was not the product of isolated, creative minds, but rather the logical development of a movement that sought to look at contemporary society through a vision of what the Church might be. It also suggests – to me – that this remains a powerful and radical vision still, contrary to the temptation of some Labour historians practically to write it out of the narrative. If this appears to be giving what seem to be conclusions before I have hardly begun the analysis, it is because I see these points rather as ways into the discussion. In the rest of this chapter, my aim is to contextualize this social theology by looking at its situation in ecclesiology, because that is where its rationale is to be found. I will do that first by looking briefly at three main sources of this tradition, though concentrating particularly on the ecclesiological vision of F. D. Maurice, and second by reinterpreting the history of Christian Socialism in that light.[13] Underlying my argument are three propositions, exposition of which in itself is largely beyond the scope of this chapter: first, that though the Anglican tradition of social theology has a very distinct 'English' face, it also has roots and context in the whole history of European Christianity, and in particular with the problems of European Christianity in the nineteenth century; second, that Christian Socialism in the hands of Maurice, Gore and others was nothing in fact other than applied ecclesiology, and not some sort of religious 'take' on socialism; and third, that one cannot in this sense be too preoccupied with ecclesiology, for ecclesiology and Christian doctrine are completely inseparable. But the main point of my re-reading is to refocus attention on the implications of this tradition for the local community, and to show it as an innovative and creative tradition.

---

13 In what follows, I am drawing substantially on J. Morris, *F. D. Maurice and the Crisis of Christian Authority*, Oxford: Oxford University Press, 2005.

Anglican Social Theology: An Ecclesiology of Community

If we search back through history for the many and varied
roots of this Anglican tradition of social theology, the results
will take us to some surprising places. The conventional narrative put forward by historians of nineteenth-century Britain has
tended to cast the Oxford Movement in particular, and Anglo-
Catholicism in general, as essentially nostalgic and reactionary,
remote from political and social concerns, tied up in the coils of
intra-university arguments and preoccupied with arcane matters of church doctrine and liturgy. Nothing could be further
from the truth. Leaving to one side the highly complex question
of High Church identity in the early nineteenth century – for
modern scholarship, led by Peter Nockles, has recovered for us
a picture of a wide range of High Church opinion, of which the
Oxford Movement was but one aspect – the Tractarian revival
was concerned above all to reinvigorate Anglican parish life.[14]
That did not just mean liturgical renewal, and the inculcation of
religious principles, however: it also meant the entire recasting
of social relations in the community, based on the assumption
that Christian faith is in essence a social programme, for which
the theological rationale was the doctrine of the incarnation.
The Oxford historian Simon Skinner, in a monograph of remarkable astuteness, has demonstrated how Tractarian social
teaching was both conservative in its assumptions about the interdependence of social classes and the interrelations of Church
and state, and also progressive in its aspirations for the transformation of local communities. As he asserts, for the Oxford
leaders and their followers, while for political reasons and
consequences, defence of the Church 'was a means of resist-
ing the encroachment of secular agencies', socially the Church
'presented the spectacle of Christian fellowship to which secular society might look'.[15] And it was the parish above all that
embodied these aspirations. Keble's cultivation of his parish

14 P. B. Nockles, *The Oxford Movement in Context: Anglican High Churchmanship 1760–1857*, Cambridge: Cambridge University Press, 1994.

15 S. Skinner, *Tractarians and the Condition of England: The Social and
Political Thought of the Oxford Movement*, Oxford: Oxford University Press,
2004, p. 139.

of Hursley, where he ministered for over 40 years, is the one example frequently cited: not only did he build schools and churches, as one might have expected, but he also supported allotments, a parish savings bank and migration for desperate cases.[16] But the significance of Hursley is not causal, but illustrative. As Skinner comments, it is not that the example of Hursley was carried 'downwind to thousands of vicarages nationwide', but that the movement's social and pastoral ideals were 'deliberately disseminated' through published media.[17]

That is why 'Plain' or 'Parochial' sermons form such a large part of the corpus of Tractarian publications – Newman's own *Parochial and Plain Sermons* were but the most famous example of many. One of the most influential manuals on preaching was written by the Tractarian William Gresley (1801–76), who argued that a preacher had to adapt his language and style to 'the peculiarities of those whom he addresses'.[18] The Tractarian system of divinity, for all its importance as a reassertion of church principles, needed 'reasoning and analogy' to work out its implications in parishes.[19] Gresley thought the parish system was as much a divine institution as episcopacy, and therefore he, like most of the Tractarians, devoted much attention to promoting the reform and renewal of the spiritual life of parishes.[20] It is true – and Skinner acknowledges this – that the social implications of Tractarian teaching were in a sense to emerge from its preoccupation with personal salvation and devotion, rather than being flagged 'up front' as part of a programme of social renewal. This was to give Tractarian preaching a severe and ascetic edge, if nevertheless a 'plain' and pastoral one also.

---

16 Skinner, *Tractarians*, p. 146. Cf. Keble's famous remark, 'If the Church of England were to fail, it should be found in my parish': W. O. Chadwick, *The Spirit of the Oxford Movement: Tractarian Essays*, Cambridge: Cambridge University Press, 1992, p. 62.

17 Skinner, *Tractarians*, p. 142.

18 W. Gresley, *Ecclesiastes Anglicanus: Being a Treatise on the Art of Preaching, as Adapted to a Church of England Congregation*, London: Rivingtons, 1835, p. v.

19 W. Gresley, *The Necessity of Zeal and Moderation: The Present Circumstances of the Church, Enforced and Illustrated in Five Sermons Preached before the University of Oxford*, London: Rivingtons, 1839, pp. vi–vii.

20 Gresley, *Necessity of Zeal and Moderation*, p. 72.

So Gresley emphasized 'self-examination, self-discipline, regard to conscience, frequent prayer, devout communion, holy observance, and habitual watchfulness': all these things were necessary to cultivate 'that heavenly principle of faith which is the essence of the life of God in the heart of man'.[21] For Pusey, prayer, alms and fasting were a 'holy band, for which our Blessed Lord gives rules together, and which draw up the soul to Him'.[22] Yet Pusey fulminated against the evils of industrialism, and held up the Church as a model of human community and social justice.[23] The Tractarians and their followers were hardly free from the general social assumptions and prejudices that shaped their class and age, and yet within their religious ideals they were nevertheless surprisingly radical and egalitarian, espousing the abolition of obvious social distinctions within the worshipping community, including those sustained by the almost universal practice of pew rents, and emphasizing modesty in dress and the superiority of ecclesiastical discipline to social convention.

Nevertheless, the most startling and ultimately influential statement of Anglican social radicalism was to emerge from the group who surrounded F. D. Maurice in mid-century, and who first (in England, anyway) adopted the sobriquet 'Christian Socialist'; therefore it is to Maurice that we must look for a truly *social* approach. As we shall see, Maurice's social radicalism cannot be separated, though, from his ecclesiological vision. Maurice was born to Unitarian parents in Lowestoft in 1805, studied at Cambridge and later Oxford, and came into the respective social circles of Julius Hare, later archdeacon and a disciple of Coleridge, and William Gladstone. In a way, those two circles symbolized the characteristic mixture of Coleridgeanism and High Churchmanship to be encountered in his mature theology. He was received into the Church of England through adult baptism in March 1831, and most

---

21 W. Gresley, *Practical Sermons*, London: Joseph Masters, 1848, p. 56.

22 E. B. Pusey, *Sermons During the Season from Advent to Whitsuntide*, Oxford: Parker, 1848, p. 189.

23 Cf. R. W. Franklin, *Nineteenth-Century Churches: The History of a New Catholicism in Württemberg, England, and France*, New York and London: Garland, 1997, pp. 232–3.

of his active ministry was spent in London, in successive positions as Chaplain of Guy's Hospital and then Lincoln's Inn, and as a Professor of Theology at the new King's College until 1853, when he lost his chair over his controversial views on eschatology. Late in life, not long before his death in 1872, he was elected to the Knightbridge chair of Moral Philosophy at Cambridge.[24]

It is common for historians of Victorian thought to trace Maurice's interest in Chartism, political radicalism and social activism to his upbringing as the son of a Unitarian minister.[25] Clearly that must have played a part, because it was an unusual background for a prominent mid-Victorian Anglican clergyman. But it is not perhaps the best place to begin an assessment of his social thought. Instead, one has to start from his most significant work on ecclesiology, *The Kingdom of Christ*, usually read in the second edition published in 1842. The term 'kingdom theology' undoubtedly stems from the title of that book, for Maurice argued that the kingdom of Christ was an existing reality, and not merely a future goal, and as such already exercised its claims of justice and peace over the nations of the earth. But scholars rarely take seriously the subtitle, which gives an important clue to the nature of the book – *Hints to a Quaker respecting the Principles, Constitution and Ordinances of the Catholic Church*. These are 'hints' – not a systematic picture. 'Hints' suggests something that definitely exists, but which needs to be sought out in diverse and fragmented forms. And then those words 'Principles', 'Constitution' and 'Ordinances' – words that sound as if they come from political science rather than from Christian doctrine. But they are to be taken in full seriousness, implying that the catholic Church has its own distinct political and constitutional order, an order implanted in the world by God, and eternal and unchanging. There are Neoplatonic overtones to Maurice's language: the 'spiritual

---

24 The standard biography is F. Maurice, *The Life and Letters of F. D. Maurice*, 2 vols, London: Macmillan, 1884, which has never been surpassed for detail, though F. McClain, *Maurice: Man and Moralist*, London: SPCK, 1972, adds some useful information and insight.

25 Cf. O. J. Brose, *Frederick Denison Maurice: Rebellious Conformist*, Athens, OH: Ohio University Press, 1971.

constitution', as he describes it, is rather like a form or idea inherent in material reality, constituting it, shaping it, yet also correcting it and rebuking it; it is, in other words, both a moral and a metaphysical reality.[26] His study of ecclesiology aimed to draw out the elements of this 'spiritual constitution' by looking at its imprints in the world.

For Maurice, the catholicity of the Church was to be discerned in and through the Church's brokenness, and in all its various, fragmented manifestations: the Church was a central harmonious principle for the world, and in a sense the deeper meaning of the world. In another work Maurice even went so far as to say that the world 'contains the elements of which the Church is composed'. He wrote: 'In the Church these elements are penetrated by a uniting, reconciling power. The Church is, therefore, human society in its normal state; the World, that same society irregular and abnormal. The world is the Church without God; the Church is the world restored to its relation with God, taken back by Him into the state for which He created it.'[27] This is perhaps not so very far from Origen's understanding of the Church as the 'divine world-state' which, under the universal rule of the Logos, would 'constitute the true cosmos in the world'.[28]

This conception of the Church obviously raises some difficulties, not least because it could imply that all human societies and associations are incomplete unless absorbed into the Church. Maurice did not push his argument *that* far explicitly. Rather, in *The Kingdom of Christ*, he concentrated much of his argument instead on the external features – the 'ordinances' – by which the 'spiritual constitution' could be identified. These have a familiar ring – baptism, Eucharist, the catholic creeds, the Scriptures, episcopacy and a fixed or regular liturgical life. Take away that last, and essentially there are here the main

---

26 For the significance of this identification, see the very title of what some (for example, J. M. Ludlow) regarded as Maurice's finest work, *Moral and Metaphysical Philosophy*, new edn, 2 vols, London: Macmillan, 1873.

27 F. D. Maurice, *Theological Essays*, 4th edn, London: Macmillan, 1881, p. 343.

28 At least, as described in W. Pauck, 'The Idea of the Church in Christian History', *Church History*, vol. 21.3 (1952), p. 197.

points of what later came to be formulated as the Chicago–Lambeth Quadrilateral.[29] The sacraments and church order were definitely objective and effectual for Maurice, and he had no hesitation in describing them as divine. This is the side of Maurice that was so attractive to his later Anglo-Catholic followers, including most famously Michael Ramsey, who said of Maurice that 'his emphasis upon Church order springs directly from his sense of the Gospel of God'.[30] The language of constitutionalism, of order and ordinances, might reek of a certain kind of nineteenth-century political conservatism, and suggest a rather static, rigid vision underlying Maurice's apparently ecumenical ecclesiology, and I think that charge has some merit.[31] But it is worth bearing in mind that Maurice essentially sought to articulate corresponding outward and inward definitions of the Church. He identified the outward signs of catholicity in order to answer what was in effect a reflexive question – namely, given that the one Church of Christ exists among the divided bodies of Christians in the world, how and where could one find it? Even when Christians were bitterly divided over doctrine and order, Maurice suggested, elements (the 'hints' again) of the one Church could be traced in their own particular traditions. But the inward definition was equally important for him, for it rested on what could broadly be called a theology of participation in God, drawn perhaps as Donald Allchin has suggested from Maurice's rather eclectic

---

29 Maurice's conception was almost certainly influential on William R. Huntington, whose formulation in *The Church Idea* (1870) in turn influenced the General Convention of the Episcopal Church at Chicago in 1886: M. Woodhouse-Hawkins, 'Maurice, Huntington, and the Quadrilateral', in J. Robert Wright (ed.), *Quadrilateral at One Hundred*, Oxford: Forward Movement Publications, 1988. Nevertheless, Maurice's discussion itself could be said to stand in a long tradition of Anglican views, stemming back at least as far as Richard Field's *Of the Church* (1606), for which see Morris, *F. D. Maurice*, pp. 79–80.

30 A. M. Ramsey, *The Gospel and the Catholic Church*, London: Longmans Green, 1936, p. 214.

31 That seems to me part of the charge underlying John Milbank's passing comment in *The Word Made Strange*, Oxford: Blackwell, 1997, that Maurice was working within 'the "English positivist" tradition of a "discoverable divine government"' (p. 34).

reading of the Greek Fathers.[32] The Church was a fellowship of communion, in which knowledge of God – that is, participation in God's very being of love – was offered to those who trusted in him, for if God gave us grace 'not to love our lives to the death; if he makes us willing to sacrifice ourselves for His glory and the good of men, the communion [of believers with God] may become very real even here'.[33]

It would be possible to leave the analysis of Maurice's ecclesiology at this point, because it is clear from that last quote how his vision of the Church as the centre of the world and as a communion whose very being is a sharing in the communion of God drives him towards what would today be called an inclusive vision of humanity. That could be sufficient as a basis for a social theology. It was certainly an unusual emphasis in the nineteenth century. But there are three further points to make. The first takes us back to the language of constitutionalism. Maurice's idea of the Church as a constitution for humanity functioned as just one aspect of a threefold idea of human association, albeit the highest one, for alongside the Church, Maurice also conceived of the nation and the family as intrinsic aspects of God's providential and creative care.[34] I cannot deal with the family here, but the concept of nation for Maurice effectively expressed the notion of the *local* church: the one catholic Church was encountered in and through national churches. Nationality was divinely intended.[35] There was a debt here to Coleridge's *Constitution of the Church and State* (1830), with its idea of the 'opposition and necessary harmony

---

32 See A. M. Allchin, 'F. D. Maurice as Theologian', *Theology*, vol. 76.640 (1973), pp. 513–25.

33 F. D. Maurice, *The Doctrine of Sacrifice Deduced from the Scriptures*, 2nd edn, London: Macmillan, 1879, p. 241.

34 F. D. Maurice, *The Kingdom of Christ, or Hints to a Quaker Respecting the Principles, Constitution and Ordinances of the Catholic Church*, vol. 1, 4th edn, London: Macmillan, 1891, pp. 260–71.

35 It is this that led Rowan Williams to suggest that the 'whole tenor of Maurice's work is anti-pluralist and even theocratic', though this does not altogether reflect the running theme of liberty and of the partial or incomplete nature of all actual historical associations in Maurice's writings: R. D. Williams, 'Liberation Theology and the Anglican Tradition', in D. Nicholls and R. D. Williams, *Politics and Theological Identity: Two Anglican Essays*, London: Jubilee, 1984, p. 18.

of Law and Religion'.[36] For Maurice, the national Church's responsibility was therefore to, and for, the whole of society, and if we apply his conception of the Church as a communion for all, with no distinction of rank, then it is not difficult to see how and why his defence of establishment rested on a view of the Church that was capable of radical political engagement. It implied, after all, a substantial criticism of possessive individualism and the doctrine of private interests serving public ends, for, in concert with this national corporatism, Maurice could assert that 'Many writers begin with considering mankind a multitude of units ... I cannot adopt that method. At my birth, I am already in a Society.'[37]

Moreover – the second point – Maurice rooted his idea of the Church's responsibility for all in his understanding of the incarnation, which he never discussed in any systematic way but which is nevertheless a recurrent theme of his work. Again, here there was a contrast with what he took to be the dominant Evangelical conception of the life of faith as essentially a matter of individual concern. For Maurice, the affirmation of material reality in and through the incarnation contradicted the common tendency to see the life of faith as a passage through a vale of tears in hope of a better, future life after death. Rather, he affirmed a view of the Church 'as a fellowship constituted by God Himself, in a divine and human Person, by Whom it is upheld, by Whom it is preserved from the dismemberment with which the selfish tendencies of our nature are always threatening it'.[38] This fellowship was actual, and present. The doctrine of the incarnation accordingly was the engine not only of a particular understanding of the Church itself, but of the Church's vision of humanity as a fellowship of mutual love and responsibility. '[If] Christ be really the head of every man,'

---

36 Maurice, *Kingdom of Christ*, I, p. xxi.

37 F. D. Maurice, *Social Morality*, London: Macmillan, 1869, p. 24.

38 F. D. Maurice, *Christian Socialism* (1893), a pamphlet quoted in Inglis, *Churches and the Working Classes*, and in turn in C. Walsh, 'The Incarnation and the Christian Socialist Conscience in the Victorian Church of England', *Journal of British Studies*, vol. 34.3 (1995), p. 356; the title was not an original one of Maurice, and I have not yet been able to verify this quotation from work published in Maurice's lifetime.

Maurice asserted, 'and if He really [has] taken human flesh, there is ground for a universal fellowship among men ... Now the denial of a universal head is practically the denial of all communion in society.'[39] He could call the incarnation the 'kernel mystery of the universe'.[40] As the centre of history, the incarnation was both the principle through which history was to be interpreted, and the guarantee of God's gift to all humanity, regardless of class, race or gender: it showed the people of the highways that they were partakers of 'the most unspeakable privileges'.[41]

But where could one look to see this vision of communion, this incarnational praxis, embedded? This brings me to my third point, and the final one I want to make in my all-too-brief survey of Maurice's ecclesiology. Of course, the implication of all that I have said before is that Maurice thought that the polity and practice of the Church should reflect its divine constitution. But the Church of England of Maurice's day did not have any central organization to speak of – no Board for Mission and Unity, no Doctrine Commission, hardly any central bureaucracy, not even (for most of his life) a representative system of sorts, and certainly of course no Archbishops' Council. It is not clear where or how some sort of national policy could have been devised to match Maurice's social vision – even assuming he could have persuaded the hierarchy of its merits. Instead, his eyes were almost always on the severely local, the parish, which for Maurice in effect became the most important locus of the Church's national, social vocation. The true Universal Church was implied 'in the existence' of each particular church.[42] And so he took his own local, particular responsibilities with the utmost seriousness, and resisted attempts by various of his followers to persuade him to abandon or bypass his local commitments in order to head national organizations. The parish was the centre of his radical praxis. As he wrote tellingly to one of his most prominent supporters:

39 Maurice, *Life and Letters of F. D. Maurice*, vol. 2, p. 258.

40 F. D. Maurice, *What is Revelation?*, London: Macmillan, 1859, p. 102.

41 F. D. Maurice, *Lincoln's Inn Sermons, 1st series*, I, London: Macmillan, 1860, p. 199.

42 Maurice, *Lincoln's Inn Sermons*, p. 285.

[T]he Devil will not the least object to my saying the Church has a bearing upon all common life, if I take no pains that my particular Church should bear upon it at all ... Lincoln's Inn is a very powerful body of cultivated men in the midst of as bad a neighbourhood for health and probably education as most in London. If a small body of us could unite to do something for that place our bond would be surely a quasi-sacramental one – a much better one than that of any club or league.[43]

If we can see in Maurice's ecclesiology how it was possible to draw together an incarnational doctrine with a social theology, then that process was certainly carried further in the work of subsequent generations of Anglo-Catholic thinkers. The leading figure here must surely be Charles Gore. Gore, along with Henry Scott Holland and others, was one of the founders of the Christian Social Union, which promoted the study of social issues from a Christian perspective, and which came to represent a rather loose and largely non-political (or non-partisan) Christian Socialism among senior clergy of the Church of England at the end of the nineteenth century. Gore's theological importance in this respect has many strands. Influenced at Balliol College, Oxford by the school of Philosophical Idealism associated with Thomas Green (1836–82), he viewed the doctrine of the incarnation as the central principle by which the evolution of history could be understood Christianly, as was indicated by his contributions to the notorious essay collection *Lux Mundi* (1889), subtitled *A Series of Studies in the Religion of the Incarnation*. Perhaps more than anyone else, he coupled a theological and liturgical approach that was explicitly Anglo-Catholic with a commitment to a radical social theology he was prepared to call 'socialist'. He was doctrinally orthodox, or even conservative, and yet alert to the implications of modern biblical and historical criticism for traditional theology. He was not, as James Carpenter pointed out, a systematic theologian, but rather a church theologian and Christian apologist, who sought to interpret the world he experienced in Christian

43 Maurice, *Life and Letters of F. D. Maurice*, vol. 2, pp. 26–7.

terms, and to challenge his society to fulfil the Christian social vision.[44]

Gore certainly read and appreciated Maurice, though he also imbibed much from Brooke Foss Westcott's parallel but somewhat separate commitment to a Christian social thought.[45] Like Maurice, he was sceptical of the individualistic connotations of much that passed for popular theology. Unlike Maurice, however, he was prepared to countenance the organization of Christian opinion at a national level, and to use his influence, both as a theologian and then as bishop successively of Worcester, Birmingham and Oxford, to argue for a socially engaged Anglicanism. Much could be written about the nature and implications of his social theology. But it is worth noting in particular two aspects of his life and work, both of which bear on the theme of community. One was his commitment to eucharistic worship as the Church's expression of its social vision. This is made very clear right at the beginning of his discussion of eucharistic doctrine, *The Body of Christ* (1901), for there he defends his choice of title not only on the grounds that it refers to the sacrament itself, but because it also refers to 'the nature of the holy society' of which the sacrament is the 'spiritual nourishment'.[46] The full implications of this emphasis, at least in practical worship, were to await development in the twentieth century, in the liturgical movement associated in particular with the parish communion and the name of Gabriel Hebert. But we can see in essence the strong connection liturgical renewal was to make between the celebration of the Eucharist and the constitution of community already present in Gore's theology. Gore found in Patristic thought a social resonance lost altogether, he argued, from more modern conceptions: a 'miserable individualism in our thoughts of holy communion has taken the place', he claimed, 'of the rich and moving thought which in ancient days was so

---

44 J. Carpenter, *Gore: A Study in Liberal Catholic Thought*, London: Faith Press, 1960, p. 14.

45 Carpenter, *Gore*, pp. 244–5.

46 C. Gore, *The Body of Christ: An Inquiry into the Institution and Doctrine of Holy Communion*, London: John Murray, 1901, p. 1.

prominent'; a truly sacrificial manner of living, encapsulated in a 'unity of spirit and life' in our worship, should show itself in 'real brotherliness ... [and] in those habitual and considerate good works of love by which the body of Christ on earth is to be bound together'.[47] Here we have more than an echo of the Oxford Movement's conviction that liturgy and life go together, and of Maurice's sense that the implications of Christian worship and teaching are for the whole of society, and that Christians need to think outwards from the way they worship to the way they relate to others around them. We also have more than an echo, incidentally, of Continental Catholicism's twentieth-century *ressourcement*.

But Gore did not just teach about community – he also created it, or founded it. He was not a parish priest, and one looks mostly in vain in his work for the very high emphasis on the parish that we saw in William Gresley. But he did play the leading part in founding the Community of the Resurrection (CR), and like most of the Community's founders, as Alan Wilkinson tells us, he thought of it as a Christian Socialist community.[48] Practicalities surely fell far short of ideals in the implementation of this vision. Though CR has proved immensely influential in different ways throughout the twentieth century, and is associated particularly with the anti-apartheid struggle in South Africa, as well as with the ideals of the Christian Social Union, for much of the late nineteenth and early twentieth century it was essentially a group of public school and Oxbridge-educated clergy who shared many of the social prejudices of their class. Still, its attempt to re-imagine a religious order in a way that constructively responded to the social and industrial conditions of the modern world remains an engaging and relevant example, not least because in this it echoed the spirit of other newly founded Anglican communities, such as the Community of St John the Baptist, or 'Sisters of Mercy' founded at Clewer in 1852, and the Society of the Sacred Mission, founded by Herbert Kelly in 1893.

---

47 Gore, *Body of Christ*, pp. 286–7.

48 A. Wilkinson, *Christian Socialism: Scott Holland to Tony Blair*, London: SCM Press, 1998, p. 53.

What is offered above is no more than a selective sketch of aspects of the roots of modern Anglican social theology, taken from the particular perspective of High Churchmanship and Anglo-Catholicism. This is not meant to imply that other traditions within Anglicanism, and within British Christianity more widely, have had no part to play in Christian responses to the social challenges of the modern age. But it is meant, in a sense polemically, to assert the constructive and adaptive relevance of a tradition that is at risk of allowing itself to be seen as static, self-preoccupied and defensive. It is also intended as a reminder that innovation and inventiveness is not a feature of the contemporary Church alone, but an abiding aspect of the history of the Church of England in the last two centuries or more. Fuelled by their strong emphasis on the doctrine of the incarnation, Anglo-Catholics proved themselves ready to improvise new solutions to new problems, even as they asserted the authority of the ancient Church. The primary location for innovation, in practice and also in theory, was almost always the parish, for that is where the ministry of the Church was located and where the people of God could meet to offer prayer and praise. Thus the revival and renewal of eucharistic worship was definitely part of a 'social programme' for Anglo-Catholics. But they were also instrumental in developing parish missions, active in encouraging social and welfare organizations for the local community, prepared if necessary to engage socially and politically to promote the well-being of the local community, and willing in themselves (hence the mythology of the 'slum-priests') to demonstrate that 'incarnational living' which Stuart Jeffries was to find in quite a different church context decades later.

The Church and 'Christian Socialism'

Having looked selectively at the roots of the Anglo-Catholic tradition of social theology, I now continue my re-reading of this tradition by looking a little more closely at the specific phenomenon of Christian Socialism. This is a movement particularly associated with Maurice's name, and that was certainly the exemplar of his social theology, but it outgrew his rather limited conception of social and political action in the decades following his death. According to the conventional narrative it began when Maurice, together with Charles Kingsley (1819–75) and a lawyer, John Ludlow (1821–1911), were jogged into action by the failure of the Chartist movement in 1848, which in their view exposed the inability of the Church of England to understand or sympathize with the plight of working people.[49] For four years, so the conventional account runs, the three of them, together with a ragtag band of young supporters, published journals and pamphlets aimed at working people, campaigned on various welfare and employment issues, and encouraged the formation of workers' cooperatives. The events cannot be gainsaid, but as I have already implied, the context in which we have to read these initiatives from Maurice's perspective does need re-examination.

Maurice was certainly well aware of the general level of public concern over the conditions of working people in Britain in the 1830s and 1840s, and particularly of the literature of the 'Hungry Forties'. But the initiatives in which he was involved from 1848 onwards were almost all local and small-scale and related one way or another to his ministry. He started Bible classes at which working men studied alongside professionals, a night school for working men, a ragged school for poor children and a network of contacts that included various Chartist leaders.[50] Much of this effort was not all that different from the social activism of many other parish clergy. But in his writing, and in particular his various attempts at producing literature for working people, such as the short-lived journal *Politics for the People*, the connection Maurice sought to make between the alleviation of poverty and the responsibility of the national Church for the whole of society was very clear. As he said in the journal's opening issue, 'POLITICS FOR THE PEOPLE cannot

---

49 Cf. C. E. Raven, *Christian Socialism 1848–54*, new edn, London: Cass, 1968, and T. Christensen, *The Origins and History of Christian Socialism 1848–1854*, Aarhus: Universitetsforlaget, 1962.

50 Morris, *F. D. Maurice*, pp. 141–3.

be separated from Religion. They must start from Atheism, or from the acknowledgment that a Living and Righteous God is ruling in human society not less than in the natural world.'[51] And again, much of this literature was aimed equally at the Church itself, for as he said, '[if] we do not sympathize with [working men's] miseries we are not fit to discuss the remedies which they propose themselves, or which others have proposed for them'.[52] Christian Socialism – a term that Maurice finally adopted in 1850 – was not striking off in a new direction, but simply exploring more intensely and closely the implications of his ecclesiology.

That much is clear too from the more impressive efforts Maurice, Ludlow and others made in the direction of co-operation. Here again what they achieved was relatively short-lived, and mostly confined to London. Moreover, it did not make much contact with the separate, parallel movement that had begun somewhat earlier in northern England – famously in Rochdale – and which was to be more directly the genesis of the modern cooperative movement.[53] The key to the success of the Rochdale and related schemes was mutuality and common ownership by consumers; the schemes the London Christian Socialists promoted were producers' cooperatives, in many ways a much more challenging and difficult task to carry off when faced with direct competition from other, private producers. Tailors', shoemakers', builders', printers', bakers' and needlewomen's associations were created within a couple of years from 1850 under the auspices of a Central Board of management chaired by Maurice, but most of these organizations did not last more than a few years.[54] What mattered to Maurice was that the principle of association, or co-operation,

51 *Politics for the People*, no. 1, 6 May 1848.

52 *Politics for the People*, no. 1.

53 See G. D. H. Cole, *A Century of Cooperation*, London: Cooperation Union, 1944.

54 For a brief account, see Morris, *F. D. Maurice*, pp. 143–4. The most influential voice in the movement was Edward Vansittart Neale, who dedicated his life to the cause of the associations; see P. N. Backstrom, *Christian Socialism and Co-operation in Victorian England: Edward Vansittart Neale and the Co-operative Movement*, London: Croom Helm, 1974.

expressed perfectly his understanding of the mutuality of the communion of the Church. As he said, co-operation was a way of carrying out 'what seems to us the only law of fellowship among Christian men'.[55] Indeed, he even extended the principle of co-operation to the relation of the sexes.[56]

Maurice may have devised a characteristic and distinctive justification for the workers' associations, but it is also important to recognize that they echoed similar steps taken on the Continent in the 1840s, and particularly in France. John Ludlow had spent many years in France and was familiar with French radical politics, visiting Paris specifically several times between 1848 and 1850 to see the French workers' associations at first hand. Instrumental in the French movement was Philippe Joseph Benjamin Buchez (1796–1865), a former disciple of Saint-Simon who had converted to Catholicism in 1829 but who never became a practising Catholic, hoping instead to 'Christianize' French republicanism.[57] He believed that the ideals of the French Revolution were a development of the fundamental truths of Christianity, and especially of its principle of altruism. Buchez's movement undoubtedly provided some of the inspiration for Ludlow, and indirectly for Maurice. A long article on 'Practical socialism' in his 'house journal' *L'Atelier*, distinguished true, practical socialism from false, dangerous socialism, which it is clear the writer identified with theoretical socialism.[58] The expression of this practical socialism would be the principle of association, the only means by which workers could be truly free. Independent associations, relating to each other and to the state, would become the necessary social correlative to the political power achieved by enfranchising the working class. Incidentally, these 'associations' were not so dissimilar from the mediating institutions a later Anglican

---

55 F. D. Maurice, *Reasons for Co-operation: A Lecture delivered at the Office for Promoting Working Men's Associations*, London: Parker, 1851, p. 7.

56 Cf. F. D. Maurice, 'On Sisterhoods', *Victoria Magazine*, August 1863.

57 See A. Cuvillier, *P.-J. Buchez et les origines du socialisme Chrétien*, Paris: Presses universitaires de France, 1848, and J. B. Duroselle, *Les Débats du catholicisme social en France, 1822–1870*, Paris: Presses universitaires de France, 1951.

58 *L'Atelier: organ special de la classe laborieuse*, November 1848, republished, in facsimile, EDHIS, Paris, 1978, A. Corbon, 'Le socialisme pratique'.

writer, J. N. Figgis (1866–1919), was to propose as essential for the well-being of the modern democratic state.[59] The writer in *L'Atelier* conceded that this would require a higher standard of virtue from workers than was possible in a state of wage-labour, but he didn't seem to see this as an obstacle. Association was a high and demanding moral ideal.

Buchez himself showed scant interest in Britain, unlike the rest of the French Catholic press. But he shared with the Continental press the conviction that the conditions under which the poor lived in Britain were exceptionally degrading.[60] *L'Atelier*'s comment on the ill-fated Chartist meeting on Kennington Common in April 1848, at which the People's Charter and petition was paraded before being submitted to Parliament, was that, having hoped to see the dawn of a new republic, in fact the day found the people 'a mob ['une masse'] made stupid and effete ['lâche'] by the physical and moral misery in which the English aristocracy has enchained it'.[61] We can easily match this contempt for the situation of the British working class – very widespread in Continental Europe in the mid-nineteenth century – with the conviction of southern plantation owners in America that slavery, however objectionable in itself, was preferable to the conditions of the factories and the degradation of wage-labour – an argument put forward also by no less a person than Maurice's friend Thomas Carlyle.[62]

Ludlow's awareness of these Continental perspectives put him in a different place from Maurice when it came to questions of strategy. The two nearly fell out over Maurice's refusal to be drawn into supporting Ludlow's attempt to create a national workers' organization. By the mid-1850s, Maurice's interest in the workers' associations had apparently waned, and again

59 See especially J. N. Figgis, *Churches in the Modern State*, London: Longmans Green, 1913.

60 See J. N. Morris, '"Separated Brethren": French Catholics and the Oxford Movement', in S. J. Brown and P. Nockles (eds), *The Oxford Movement: Europe and the Wider World 1830–1930*, Cambridge: Cambridge University Press, 2012.

61 *L'Atelier*, 7 May 1848.

62 Cf. E. Fox Genovese and E. D. Genovese, *The Mind of the Master Class: History and Faith in the Southern Slaveholders' Worldview*, New York: Cambridge University Press, 2005; Carlyle, 'Occasional Discourse'.

most scholars have assumed that this simply demonstrates his impractical nature, and his failure to grasp the real nature of socialism.[63] The same comments have been made against the whole of the history of the Christian Socialist movement, however, and even against the broader and more amorphous phenomenon of Anglican social theology in general.[64] For all its organization and publication, the Christian Social Union seemed to be not much more than a talking shop, after all. Christian Socialist groups were notoriously small and fissiparous in the early twentieth century, and even the resurgence of the movement towards the end of the century, and its apparent apogee under Blair, has not dented much the common general impression that Christian Socialism remains a curiously wan and underdeveloped animal.

But it is too easy to sneer. In the nineteenth century, people were still groping their way cautiously towards the elaboration of coherent programmes and political and social reform, and from a twenty-first-century perspective, it is not at all clear that the collectivist approaches adopted by state welfarism in place of voluntary action were the inevitable and successful solutions they were assumed to be in 1945. It is no accident that, across Europe, and in the United States, the challenges of industrialization and the intellectual legacy of the Enlightenment and the political inheritance of the more radical and anti-religious aspects of the French Revolutionary tradition were putting enormous strains on the Christian churches. One possible way forward was the Ultramontane way, the institutionalization of resistance to change through a highly centralized ecclesial system that was itself, paradoxically, an echo of the authoritarian, bureaucratized methods of the modern state. Another way was what eventually came to be called 'fundamentalism' (though not until the early twentieth century). The Christian Socialists were trying precisely not to commit themselves to any strategy

63 This is the constant theme of E. R. Norman, *The Victorian Christian Socialists*, Cambridge: Cambridge University Press, 1987.

64 See E. R. Norman, *Church and Society in England 1770–1970: A Historical Study*, Oxford: Clarendon Press, 1976, especially chapter 6, 'Christian Social Ideals, 1900–1920', pp. 221–78.

that would leave the Church stranded, wrapped up in its own affairs. They sought the transformation of the Church, not through a centralized campaign, but by its reinvigoration at local level.

Conclusion

It is a mistake to judge the tradition of social theology that Maurice and others came to represent from the standard of a conception of socialism as a material philosophy that one encounters again and again in the literature of the modern labour movement. Nor is it persuasive, I think, to bracket it with 'ethical socialism', a term that is almost always used in a pejorative way, as if a falling away from the harder-edged, 'gold' standard of Marxist economics. So I reiterate that the only place in which one can effectively read Anglican social theology is in the context of ecclesiology. It is perhaps best thought of as 'applied ecclesiology'. In the case of Anglo-Catholicism, it was an attempt to work out the implications of convictions about the incarnation and about the divine constitution of the Church as a union or communion of human beings as a prophetic corrective to a Church that had bought too easily into moral and economic individualism. Maurice constantly reminded his readers, and his hearers, that Christian faith was for the world, as God had made the world: its message, its value, was universal, and could not be wrapped up in a 'private sphere'. His later followers, such as Stewart Headlam, Thomas Hancock and Conrad Noel, drew out this conclusion even more forcefully. Headlam, for example, drew from Maurice the lesson that the incarnation established the brotherhood of men, and that 'punishment, ruin, loss, damnation, Hell, inevitably and always in the long run await the nation which ignores the great principle of brotherhood'.[65] And as Noel was to put it, 'politics, in the wider sense of social justice, are part and parcel of the gospel of Christ and to ignore them is to be false to His

---

65 S. Headlam, in *The Meaning of the Mass* (1896), as quoted in Walsh, 'The Incarnation and the Christian Socialist Conscience', p. 368.

teaching ... [W]orship divorced from social righteousness is an abomination to God.'[66]

It was in fact these later figures, including not only disciples of Maurice, but also more independent voices such as Gore and Westcott, who crystallized and radicalized earlier arguments, and in the process fusing them into something more like an explicitly Anglo-Catholic view. Headlam in particular took what were admittedly existing arguments in Maurice's work, but which he did not especially emphasize, and in effect codified them. He drew out Maurice's teaching on communion, the kingdom and the Eucharist, and made of it a eucharistic social theology, for – as he said in *The Meaning of the Mass* (1901), for example – the social responsibility of all Christians was one that 'the weekly administration of the great Emancipator's Supper intensifies, while it gives us, thank God, the strength to comply with it: the responsibility for each one of us ... to think out, and try and find out, what are the evils which are preventing our England from being the veritable Kingdom of Heaven upon earth'.[67] So Maurice's social theology in effect stimulated two strands that ran through the Church of England in the late nineteenth and twentieth centuries – one, the catholic, Christian Socialism of the Guild of St Matthew, the Church Socialist League and other bodies; and the other, the less distinctly 'Anglo-Catholic' social theology of the Christian Social Union, the Christian Socialist movement of today, of William Temple and R. H. Tawney and others.[68] Whatever their differences in the end, both shared common roots in Maurice's ecclesiology, as well as in the theological ideals of the Oxford Movement. It is precisely because Maurice's idea of Christian Socialism was not merely a watered-down version of a secular socialist ideal, nor a mere baptism of it, but a view springing out of, and fully consistent with, his ecclesiology, that it remains relevant today.

---

66 S. Dark (ed.), *Conrad Noel: An Autobiography*, London: Dent, 1945, p. 91.

67 As quoted in Walsh, 'The Incarnation and the Christian Socialist Conscience', p. 369.

68 P. D. A. Jones, *The Christian Socialist Revival 1877–1914: Religion, Class and Social Conscience in Late Victorian England*, Princeton: Princeton University Press, 1968.

But it is also because the Anglo-Catholic tradition of social criticism and social thought always was, ineluctably, a tradition grounded in particular practices of worship and prayer, which sought to unite liturgy and society in a vision of community practice responsive to the social challenges of modern Britain. It wasn't as daft as suggesting that the solution to poverty was incense. Rather, it tried to express a correspondence of belief and practice, such that the behaviour of the Christian community towards the most vulnerable in the community would reflect exactly the spirit in which God himself is worshipped. This was put memorably by Frank Weston, Bishop of Zanzibar, to the Anglo-Catholic Congress of 1923: 'You cannot claim to worship Jesus in the Tabernacle if you do not pity Jesus in the slum.'[69] It was a tradition of experimentation, out of traditional concerns. But it was also a tradition of community action, in which the Eucharist could serve as a powerful metaphor for building up the fellowship of the whole Christian community, as well as a means by which it could be sustained.

---

69 Quoted in Norman, *Church and Society in England*, p. 234.

3

Inculturation – Faithful to the Past: Open to the Future

JAMES HEARD

And the Word became flesh and lived among us, and we have seen his glory.

These are some of the most well-known words in the Bible – the Word becomes flesh and 'tabernacled' [εσκηνωσεν εν ημιν] among us. It describes God becoming incarnate in the life and world of first-century Palestine, as a Jewish, Aramaic-speaking male, yet within a world where Greek was the common language in use and Imperial Rome was the occupying power. This is the particular world into which God became incarnate. It is a long way from the world of eternal timeless truths about God's essence that has featured so prominently in the Western tradition.

This 'enfleshed' or sacramental faith is expressed bodily in the worshipping life of the Church, which recognizes that: 'A human being is not just a reasoning mind, much less a mass of emotion. We are body-soul creatures ...'[1] It is such theology that underpins what it is to be Christian, and it determines the shape of worship, ecclesiology and mission.

This chapter will reflect upon a missiological theme – inculturation. Inculturation expresses a generous ecclesiology, because it lays great stress on being carefully and respectfully

---

1 J. D. Crichton, 'A Theology of Worship', in Cheslyn Jones, Geoffrey Wainwright, Edward Jarnold SJ and Paul Bradshaw (eds), *The Study of Liturgy*, London: SPCK, 1992, p. 12.

attentive to the missional context. One of its main challenges lies in the necessary tension involved between fidelity to the past *and* responding creatively to the cultural context in which an ecclesial community finds itself. I shall begin by locating the roots of inculturation within the early Church. Some of its main features will be highlighted along with its challenges, and the various recent tensions that have arisen in its practice.

Early Church

It is instructive to begin by noting the contextual nature of the early Church. What is clear is that conflict was experienced from the very beginning. One of the issues was the conversion of proselytes and pagan Gentiles, which raised very difficult issues. The group of early followers of 'The Way' had to decide to what degree one had to become Jewish to be a disciple of Christ. The New Testament writers often drew upon the tradition they knew – their Jewish heritage – to theologically unravel their experience of Christ. When they were eventually expelled from synagogues, this Jewish tradition shaped their liturgy.[2]

Andrew Walls notes that with an openness to the Holy Spirit, the tradition of the Church evolved in ways that 'must have seemed to old-style Jewish believers to be dangerous, uncharted territory'. After 'much debate' (Acts 15.7), the Jerusalem council viewed converts not as Jewish proselytes, who were expected to be circumcised and to keep the Torah, but as Greek converts. It was their calling to open up the ways of thinking, speaking and acting, characteristic of Hellenistic society in the Roman East Mediterranean, to the influence of Christ. And Christ could not be formed among them while they insisted on patterning themselves on Jewish believers, even exemplary Jewish believers. The prophetic challenge of the gospel required a conversion in which every aspect of Hellenistic life

2 In *The Search for the Origins of Christian Worship*, London: SPCK, 2002, pp. 21–46, Paul Bradshaw cites elements of synagogue liturgy, the daily practice of prayer, forms of prayer themselves, and grace at meals. The Temple cult imagery figured in liturgical practice from the fourth century onwards.

and all its institutions had to be turned towards Christ. Walls notes the experimental nature of this evolving tradition: 'there were no precedents; the guideposts familiar to early believers were there no longer. Christ would be made flesh once more, made manifest where he had not walked in flesh before, as he was received by faith in Hellenistic society.'[3]

Tom Smail highlights the creative role of the Holy Spirit in the process of inculturation: 'It is helpful to think of the Spirit much more personally and creatively as an artist whose one subject is the Son, and who is concerned to paint countless portraits of that subject on countless human canvases using the paints and brushes provided by countless human cultures and historical situations.'[4] Each new cultural and historical situation brought a whole variety of ways the Church was called to be.

In short, the Christian faith evolved in a way that was profoundly contextual, which means that one cannot draw a 'blueprint ecclesiology' from the tumultuous world of the early followers of Christ.[5] Further, this challenges the notion of a 'pure' gospel that is effectively *a*-cultural and *trans*-cultural, which only risks dilution by being radically contextualized or shaped for a particular agenda.[6] Such an understanding provides the basis for thinking how the gospel might be inculturated today.

Inculturation

The term 'inculturation' has been used in Christian missiology to refer to the adaptation of the gospel in particular cultures being evangelized, although, as highlighted above, it is hardly

3 Andrew Walls, 'Converts or Proselytes? The Crisis over Conversion in the Early Church', *International Bulletin*, vol. 28.1 (2004), pp. 2–6.

4 Tom Smail, *The Giving Gift*, London: Hodder & Stoughton, 1988, p. 77.

5 Nicholas Healy critiques the tendency in ecclesiology to reflect upon the Church in abstraction from its concrete identity and thus to present idealized accounts of the Church. N. Healy, *Church, World and the Christian Life: Practical-Prophetic Ecclesiology*, Cambridge: Cambridge University Press, 2000.

6 Martyn Percy, *The Salt of the Earth*, London: Sheffield Academic Press, 2001, p. 50.

a new phenomenon. For example, Paul's presentation in the synagogue at Antioch (Acts 13) was profoundly different from his speech to the Greeks at the Areopagus (Acts 17).

Contextualization involves a greater focus on the cultural context where the Christian faith is to take root and expression.[7] As Pope Paul VI put it, it is about transposing the gospel into a language that is 'anthropological and cultural', rather than 'semantic or literary', and to evangelize cultures 'not in a purely decorative way, as it were, by applying a thin veneer, but in a vital way, in depth and right to their very roots'.[8] The importance of a dialectical process of reciprocal and respectful listening, of journeying together, is stressed.

Bevans and Schroeder note that the primary task in inculturation is to be in *dialogue* with the context in which the gospel is to be lived out and 'to *listen* and *discern* how best to connect the unchanging aspects of faith with the changing and challenging aspects of a particular experience, culture, social location or social changes in a specific place or within a specific people'. Second, they note not all things in culture are good. Certain aspects of a culture need to be challenged. Inculturation is thus done best in 'prophetic dialogue'.[9]

Further, there is a reciprocal dimension to this. Lesslie Newbigin suggests that the visible community did not simply *absorb* converts, and the early Church was challenged by what the Holy Spirit was doing in them in quite radical ways. The lesson from Peter's experience with Cornelius (Acts 10) was that the Church had to be open to learning things about its own identity in a way it could never have anticipated in advance.[10] The

---

7 For a discussion of the various 'levels' of contextualization – translation, adaptation and inculturation – see Louis J. Luzbetak, *The Church and Cultures: New Perspectives in Missiological Anthropology*, Maryknoll, NY: Orbis Books, 1988, and Robert J. Schreiter, *Constructing Local Theologies*, Maryknoll, NY: Orbis Books, 1986.

8 *Evangelii Nuntiandi* 63, 20: www.vatican.va/holy_father/paul_vi/apost_exhortations/documents/hf_p-vi_exh_19751208_evangelii-nuntiandi_en.html (accessed 1 September 2006).

9 Stephen B. Bevans and Roger P. Schroeder, *Constants in Context: A Theology of Mission for Today*, Maryknoll, NY: Orbis Books, 2011, p. 387.

10 Lesslie Newbigin, 'Conversion', in S. Neill and G. H. Anderson (eds), *Concise Dictionary of the Christian World Mission*, London: SCM Press, 1969.

transformation of these new disciples by the Holy Spirit acted as a prophetic challenge to the existing community. The outcome was culturally and intellectually dynamic, creative and innovative.

In practice, inculturation is complex: mistakes are frequently made, but these are often only seen with the benefit of hindsight. One of the chief challenges is the possibility of syncretism – of the Church 'going native' and losing its prophetic voice.

Challenges of Inculturation

There have been various daring attempts by Jesuit missionaries to connect with culture, including Roberto de Nobili in South India. His approach contrasted starkly with what followed, of 'colonial evangelization', where there was no dialogue, no mutual listening and no reciprocal learning.[11] The latter was a missionary methodology where indigenous culture was deliberated undermined.[12]

De Nobili had a more positive view of Indian culture. He viewed the caste system as a benign social institution and himself lived the life of a high-caste Indian in respect of food, clothing and such customs as the wearing of the sacred thread. Caste segregation is now considered unacceptable. Yet there are still churches in South Asia who have separate chalices for Dalits. And while later generations viewed de Nobili's approach to caste as unacceptable, other customs that the Franciscan missionaries had condemned as heathen have been accepted as harmless by later generations of Indian Christians.[13]

---

11 Hiebert describes the period between 1800 and 1950 as the 'era of noncontextualization' for Protestant missions, in which it was thought that a singular Western culture simply had to be indigenized without surrendering any of its essence (in David J. Bosch, *Transforming Mission: Paradigm Shifts in the Theology of Mission*, Maryknoll, NY: Orbis, 1991, p. 427).

12 Aylward Shorter, *Evangelization and Culture*, London: Geoffrey Chapman, 1994, p. 29.

13 Lesslie Newbigin, *The Gospel in a Pluralist Society*, London: SPCK, 1989, pp. 142–3.

The challenge of syncretism is present to a greater or lesser degree in every form of Christianity from New Testament times. Inculturation implies a continual struggle with syncretism, with the elements of culture that are incompatible with the gospel.[14] As complex as contextualization is, Shorter notes, de-syncretization enters into the definition of inculturation itself. What is clear is that fear of syncretism should not be invoked as a reason for postponing inculturation.[15]

Until relatively recently, the significance of inculturation, along with disciplines like anthropology, was thought best left to exotic tribes found in places like South America or South Asia. However, the relevance of inculturation has discovered fertile soil in pluralist Western cultures. One of the best-known books among ordinands is *Christianity Rediscovered*, written by Vincent Donovan, a Roman Catholic missionary priest. He describes the journey he embarked upon in his attempt to engage the Masai tribe with the gospel. It required the double task of listening to the gospel and culture. On his return to the United States, Donovan found American youth 'one of the most exotic tribes of all'. They had their own dress, music, rituals, language and values, all remarkably similar from New York to California. A university student advised Donovan: 'In working with young people in America, do not try to call them back to where they were, and do not try to call them to where you are, as beautiful as that place might seem to you. You must have the courage to go with them to a place that neither you nor they have ever been before.'[16]

What Donovan discovered was a plurality of cultures within his native North American home. The same is true of modern Britain. A generous ecclesiology means the Church being attentive to today's plurality of cultures and contexts, and thus being true to its catholic vocation by expressing the ολος, welcoming the *whole* in all its diversity.

---

14 Two key questions for *MSC* are whether it sufficiently challenges a rampant consumerist culture, and to what degree it encourages a transcendence of relational homogeneity.

15 Shorter, *Evangelization*, p. 152.

16 Vincent J. Donovan, *Christianity Rediscovered: An Epistle from the Masai*, London: SCM Press, 1993, p. vii.

While recognizing the contextual nature of all theology, there is also the Christian faith, the 'universal and context-transcending dimensions of theology',[17] that needs to be respected to remain authentically Christian. This is expressed in the 'rule of faith', the faith 'which has been believed everywhere, always, by all'[18] and is the common source of Catholicism, Eastern Orthodoxy and Protestantism. For example, while there are differing views within the Church about the when and how of baptism, the rite of baptism is paradigmatic for Christian initiation.

In short, how might the beliefs and practices of a generous missional Church be configured so as to relate continuity and change. This is a necessary tension and it has been described in various ways. Bretherton notes a continuity and discontinuity, between '*homeostasis* (the ability to maintain an equilibrium and to rearrange itself so as to keep things steady) with *morphogenesis* (the ability to grow, change shape, and adapt without breaking apart)'. Like an immune system, staying healthy involves a balance between the two so as to enable both maintenance and growth.[19] Stephen Bevans' and Roger Schroeder's book title, *Constants in Context*, expresses a similar theme. Christian mission, they argue, needs to be anchored in fidelity to the past – to preserve, defend and proclaim the *constants* of the Church's tradition. Yet Christian mission must also be responsive to the demands of the gospel in particular *contexts*, and be continually reinventing itself as it struggles with and approaches new situations, new peoples, new cultures and new questions. It requires openness to what is new and surprising, and a readiness to respond creatively and boldly to the *context* in which it finds itself.[20]

---

17 Bosch, *Transforming Mission*, p. 427.

18 St Vincent of Lérins, A Commonitory, in Philip Schaff and Henry Wace (eds), *Sulpitius Severus, Vincent of Lerins, John Cassian*, Peabody, MA: Hendrickson, 1995, p. 132.

19 Luke Bretherton, 'Beyond the Emerging Church?', in A. Walker and L. Bretherton (eds), *Remembering Our Future: Explorations in Deep Church*, Milton Keynes: Paternoster Press, 2007, p. 51.

20 Bevans and Schroeder, *Constants in Context*, pp. 1, 31.

There are numerous examples of how this tension is mani-
fested. The tendency has been for churches with an explicit
institutional basis to dominate the local, from which inculturation originates. Despite the Vatican II emphasis on inculturation,
it has more often collapsed when put into practice. For example, African liturgical innovations are constantly crushed by the
Roman Curia. Shorter notes that (the then Cardinal) Ratzinger
was known for his nervousness about inculturation, following Pius XII and the pre-conciliar Church, which favoured the
idea of a monolithic hybrid Christian culture, in which the
cultural matrix was Western. He highlights a sharp contrast
between the official affirmations and the Magisterium's return
to centralization and authoritarianism.[21] This raises the issue of
power, which is clearly one-sided in the way it denies any sub-
stantive change to the institution's core beliefs and practices.

Yet the imperialism of a single Western Christian culture
in the Church contradicts its vocation of catholicity. As Jonathan Clark points out (in Chapter 8), the inclusive nature of
the Church includes the ability to see the catholic Church in
diverse and new places, even in forms of worship and belief we
might find embarrassing or distasteful.[22]

The tension – between fidelity to the past and responsiveness
to new contexts – has been revealed more recently within the
Anglican tradition; between those who desire, quite rightly, to
remain faithful to the Anglican heritage, and those who have
attempted, as the Declaration of Assent affirms, to 'proclaim
that faith afresh in each generation'. The former is seen in the
book *FTP*, the latter in *MSC*. A generous ecclesiology requires
attention to both dimensions.

---

21 Shorter, *Evangelization*, p. 90.

22 The Vietnamese American theologian Peter Phan argues that inculturation would benefit greatly from a broader appreciation of popular religion,
the religion of ordinary women and men (in Bevans and Schroeder, *Constants
in Context*, p. 387). This is a dimension that is discussed by Brutus Green in
Chapter 4.

Fidelity to the Anglican Heritage

Asking what it means to remain faithful to the Church's heritage entails a reflection on ecclesiology. While there are bound to be differences of language, context and culture, what are the constants that mark the Church in its missionary outreach? Andrew Walls highlights two – Christology and ecclesiology.[23] The person of Jesus Christ (along with the relation to the Father and the Holy Spirit) has ultimate significance. There is also the importance of the Bible, the dominical sacraments, the consciousness of continuity with Israel from which the Christian phenomena had sprung, along with the act of corporate worship and prayer (a threatened one in (post) modern individualist culture). 'While the content of these constants is not the same, Christianity is never without faith in and theology of Jesus Christ and never without a commitment to and understanding of the community it names church.'[24]

What might fidelity mean for the Anglican tradition? However passionate one might, and should, be about mission, careful attention must be given to the Anglican heritage. And this is not about dead traditionalism.[25] The Church's history, liturgy and way of being should not be viewed as merely a cultural 'husk' that must be discarded on the altar of missional pragmatism. For the purpose of brevity, I shall highlight just two dimensions – institution and liturgy – because these have posed particular challenges in mission.[26]

---

23 Walls cited in Bevans and Schroeder, *Constants in Context*, p. 33.

24 Bevans and Schroeder, *Constants in Context*, p. 33. They highlight an additional four: questions of eschatology, the nature of salvation, anthropology, human culture. They use these six constants of mission as a framework to reflect on the theology of mission.

25 Jaroslav Pelikan's well-known phrase is a helpful reminder: 'Tradition is the living faith of the dead; traditionalism is the dead faith of the living. Tradition lives in conversation with the past, while remembering where we are and when we are and that it is we who have to decide. Traditionalism supposes that nothing should ever be done for the first time, so all that is needed to solve any problem is to arrive at the supposedly unanimous testimony of this homogenized tradition.' Interview in *U.S. News & World Report*, 26 July 1989.

26 The Chicago–Lambeth Quadrilateral, of course, has been a defining feature in contemporary Anglican ecclesiology.

Institution

Among those engaged in mission, there is often a frustration with the Church as an institution. Sadly, there are often well-founded reasons. For the Anglican priest David Prior, the present (institutional) structures both 'deaden and divide'.[27] Pete Ward argues for a 'liquid church' that is firmly located in the consumer nature of society. Because 'solid church' has a decreased ability to engage in genuine mission, 'the static monolith of the congregation is replaced by a dynamic inclusive and fluid dance of intimate communication'.[28]

There have been some groups in the emerging Church that seek to dispense with institution altogether. This presents a false dichotomy between institution and faith, the Church and mission. One of the consequences of a frail ecclesiology is a downgrading of the importance of the institutional life of the Church. As the Anglican doctrinal report *We Believe in the Holy Spirit* observes: 'Openness to change, vitality, warmth and surprise all need to be balanced by continuity, regularity, stability and rationality. In other words, structure and form are as important as the living content; both should be understood as the work of the one and the same Spirit.'[29]

Yet as Tom Greggs highlights (in Chapter 6), the Church as institution does not simply exist for itself but rather it exists for the world, as a servant for mission. The challenge is to hold together the dynamic and experiential element of being Christian as expressed within the worshipping life of the Church, which is enabled by its rather sober (but essential) institutional structures. This means an affirming yes to a passion for Christian renewal and direct engagement with the missional imperative and also a yes to clergy, liturgy and sacred places of worship.

---

27 In *MSC*, p. 47.

28 Pete Ward, *Liquid Church*, Carlisle: Paternoster Press, 2002, pp. 29, 55–6.

29 *We Believe in the Holy Spirit*, London: Church House Publishing, 1991, p. 55. See also Miroslav Volf in *After Our Likeness: The Church as the Image of the Trinity*, Grand Rapids: Eerdmans, 1998, pp. 234ff. Drawing upon the sociologists Peter Berger and Thomas Luckmann, he argues that every social unit is already an institution.

A high degree of reflexivity is required here because, as Miroslav Volf puts it, 'the question is not *whether* the church is an institution, but rather *what kind* of institution it is'.[30] This is of particular challenge to evangelical missiology, which tends to be activist and thus can all too easily be loosed from ecclesial moorings, to take on a life of its own and become something that exists outside of the Church.[31] This is sometimes expressed in terms like 'getting back to the NT church'. Such a perspective expresses a 'disincarnate' docetic perspective that lacks reflectivity about its own unarticulated ecclesiology.

It is also a challenge for catholic mission. It is sobering to note that Donovan's pioneering work did not continue when he left East Africa because it failed to be sufficiently connected to the wider Church.[32] Connection to the institution through parochial, diocesan and national dimensions is essential in providing accountability, support and training for the leaders, and so that such groups do not die out when the leader moves on.

Liturgy

The weekly repetition of the liturgy may feel boring. Timothy Radcliffe quotes the teenager who likened attendance at the Eucharist to sitting through an endlessly repeated film, the outcome of which is always known. He suggests that the mistake here lies in overlooking not just what Cardinal Newman called 'God's noiseless work', but human nature itself.[33]

Liturgy gives people space to think, question, journey and inhabit the tradition. More formal liturgical services avoid intensity or pressure and they are less likely to be dominated by

---

30 Volf, *After Our Likeness*, p. 234.

31 Andrew Walker, 'Deep Church as Paradosis: On Relating Scripture and Tradition', in Walker and Bretherton (eds), *Remembering Our Future: Explorations in Deep Church*, p. 63.

32 Shorter, *Evangelization*, p. 85. He suggests that Donovan did not consider the Masai's place in a Catholic communion that is visibly and hierarchically structured, and which guarantees a bond of faith, sacrament and ministry among all in the local church (p. 108).

33 Timothy Radcliffe, *Why Go to Church?*, London: Continuum, 2008, p. 6.

the personality of a charismatic leader. Its connection to the Church's yearly calendar is essential to provide breadth and balance to one's journey of faith. Radcliffe writes: 'the liturgy works in the depths of our minds and hearts a very gradual, barely perceptible transformation of who we are, so quietly that we might easily think that nothing is happening at all. The Eucharist is an emotional experience, but usually a discreet one.'[34]

This perhaps provides a prophetic challenge to a culture obsessed with novelty.[35] Yet at the parent and toddler groups at my church, children love the little rituals – for example, singing 'we light the candle [read the Bible etc.] when we go to church'. And at the other end of life, when visiting those from the parish with dementia, the liturgy of a home communion service often taps into the long-term memory of those familiar prayers they have known and come to cherish over a lifetime.

Whatever one makes of Fresh Expressions of church, a lot of its energy has come from dissatisfaction with a modernist, rational and primarily word-focused form of faith. Many groups have heeded the admonishment of Andrew Walker, who draws from his decades-long research into the charismatic movement: 'Mission shaped churches and emerging churches for all their resourcefulness, vigour and imaginative drive, will not succeed unless they heed the lessons from their charismatic precursors in renewal and drop anchors in the deep waters of a church that goes all the way down to the hidden reservoirs of the life-giving Spirit.'[36]

Many 'emerging' expressions of churches have found nourishment in creatively embracing symbol and ritual, and drawing from the deep resources of the Catholic and Ortho-

---

34 Radcliffe, *Why Go to Church?*, p. 6.

35 In *Natural Symbols*, London: Routledge, 2003, anthropologist Mary Douglas describes the loss of ritual that has led to the private internalizing of religious experience. This trend includes: 'a denunciation not only of irrelevant rituals, but of ritualism as such; exaltation of the inner experience and denigration of its standardized expressions; preference for intuitive and instant forms of knowledge; rejection of mediating institutions, rejection of any tendency to allow habit to provide the basis of a new symbolic system' (p. 21).

36 Walker, 'Deep Church as Paradosis', p. 20.

dox tradition. Doug Gay tells the story of a youth community project in Belfast involving a trip to the local Roman Catholic church followed by a visit to the Presbyterian church. As the young people filed in, one young Catholic boy looked around in surprise and asked: 'When were you robbed?'[37] It led him on a journey that involved 'auditing', 'retrieval', 'unbundling', 'supplementing' and 'remixing'.

While being highly supportive of such renewed interest in embodying the faith and drawing upon the rich heritage of the Church, the danger here is 'ecclesial bricolage', a kind of ec-clesiological potluck supper, without sufficient attention given to what it means to be a part of a tradition.[38] Further, without a rootedness in a tradition, there is a tendency to omit the less comfortable sections of the liturgy. Services can be little more than signs of self-expression in theology and style. Conversely, holding to a reciprocal dynamic, is it possible for the wider Church's liturgy to be enriched by these local, and often very creative, expressions?[39]

Today's Missional Context

Linda Woodhead's recent research, *Religion and Change in Modern Britain*, identifies various shifts in the religious land-scape.[40] She argues that there is no question of a 'return' of religion (contra Micklethwait and Wooldridge);[41] religion never really went away. Rather, it emerged after the 1980s in signifi-cantly different forms. While state churches have suffered the

---

37 Doug Gay, *Remixing the Church: Towards an Emerging Ecclesiology*, London: SCM Press, 2011, p. 1.

38 Bretherton, 'Beyond the Emerging Church?', p. 46. See also *FTP*, pp. 108–13.

39 Carl Turner helpfully writes about some of the challenges of introducing liturgical innovation, 'Liturgical Issues and Fresh Expressions', in Steven Croft and Ian Mobsby (eds), *Fresh Expressions in the Sacramental Tradition*, London: Canterbury Press, 2009, pp. 140–55.

40 Linda Woodhead and Rebecca Catto (eds), *Religion and Change in Modern Britain*, London: Routledge, 2012.

41 See John Micklethwait and Adrian Wooldridge, *God is Back: How the Global Rise of Faith is Changing the World*, London: Penguin, 2004.

most dramatic decline in power and influence, new forms of minority religion have been growing. The most vibrant and fastest growing forms of religion are those that have embraced the opportunities of the market and new media and the imperative of personal decision: from charismatic forms of Christianity to alternative forms of spirituality. She writes, 'The new entrants to the spiritual marketplace are more focused on supporting individuals in their everyday lives, fostering new kinds of identity and lifestyle, and linking the like-minded and life-hearted to one another in a vast plurality of different forms of religious alliance.'[42] The result is the mixed religious economy in which we find ourselves today. And in the midst of it all, secular voices try to defend their territory. It leaves a situation that is diverse, complex, multi-layered and contradictory.

One response to a consumerist postmodern post-Christian culture is to look to the liturgy of the pre-modern – the 're-trieval of the medieval'. Here the inherited forms of church are sites of radical resistance and are deeply relevant precisely in their nonconformity to contemporary culture.[43] The danger here is stressing a strong sense of discontinuity between the Church and culture in a search for, what Healy calls, a 'blueprint ecclesiology', or a supermodel of the Church – viewing it as the source of all truth, salvation and culture. While this holds on to an important prophetic distance, there is a lack of true mutuality and reciprocity in such a perspective. Healy writes, 'contextual ecclesial praxis informs ecclesiology, and ecclesiology informs contextual ecclesial praxis in a hermeneutical circle'.[44]

Of course, it is true that, at its best, worship can be powerful, 'a window into heaven'. Michael Sadgrove, Dean of Durham, writes: 'Worship is one of the best tools for evangelism we have. Cathedrals invest so heavily in this because there is a "converting" quality to liturgy when words, silence, music,

---

42 Woodhead and Catto, *Religion and Change in Modern Britain*, p. 27.

43 Bretherton, 'Beyond the Emerging Church?', p. 41. See also Jonathan Clarke, 'Postmodernism and Sacramentalism', in Croft and Mobsby, *Fresh Expressions in the Sacramental Tradition*, pp. 100–13.

44 Nicholas Healy, *Church, World and the Christian Life: Practical-Prophetic Ecclesiology*, Cambridge: Cambridge University Press, 2000, p. 36.

ritual actions and architecture combine to create a theatre of the soul that speaks of the holiness and love of God.'[45]

Richard Coles, from the successful 1980s pop group The Communards, describes his experience when he walked in to St Alban's, Holborn, after six months of drug-fuelled partying: 'It was full-on smells and bells. I loved that: it was like going to the opera. I can remember at the consecration the sun was coming in through the window, catching the incense rising. Then the bell rang, and it just got to me. Something just released in me. I wept. I knew I was hungry for what this was. I went in a spectator and came out a participant.'[46]

The experience of Richard Coles connected with him partly because he was raised within the Anglican tradition. But for most people who are coming from a completely non-churched background, the threshold into the liturgical richness of a church service is too big a leap. My experience of a Christmas morning Eucharistic Anglo-Catholic service several years ago illustrates this. While I found the whole experience enriching, the family who had wandered in and sat next to me seemed to find it alienating. The two teenage daughters nervously giggled throughout the service and quickly left as the congregation went forward for communion.

The challenge for today's Church is how to make connection with the non-churched, with those who are spiritually open, but who are unlikely ever to set foot in a church. There are also those who may be attracted to Jesus Christ, but find participation in a parish church too foreign. It may be due to a general mistrust of institutions. The difficulty might be cultural, theological or to do with lifestyle or personal circumstances. This, quite rightly, was the concern of *MSC*. Reflecting upon the Anglican Church in Britain today, Rowan Williams writes: 'In all kinds of places the parochial system is working remarkably. It's just that we are increasingly aware of the contexts where it simply isn't capable of making impact, where something has to

---

45 Cited in Paul Bayes and Tim Sledge (eds), *Mission-Shaped Parish: Traditional Church in a Changing Context*, London: Church Publishing House, 2009, p. 96.

46 Richard Coles, *Church Times*, 11 February 2011.

grow out of it or alongside it, not as a rival ... but as an attempt to answer questions that the parish system was never meant to answer.'[47]

Of course, chaplaincies to prisons, armed forces, schools, universities and hospitals have worked alongside the parish for centuries. More recent attempts have also been made to bridge the gap or form church in the church–world hybrid spaces and networks in which people live.[48] The consistent challenge to network or affinity groups is that they are largely homogeneous and thus do not fully express what it means to be the body of Christ, where racial, social, gender and age distinctions are transcended (Galatians 3.28). Arguably, it is right to question whether affinity groups on their own are a full expression of church. But might affinity groups be viewed as 'ecclesial groups' or 'missional expressions' that are both affirmed and supported by the institutional Church and seen as part of the wider local (that is, diocesan) church?

It is the parish that is profoundly contextual. For all its faults, the parochial model of the Church of England has – unlike almost every other social institution – maintained at least a presence where there are conditions of severe economic hardship, notably in the inner city.[49] It is the parochial model that may hold together the many expressions of the Church's life: Mothers' Union, youth groups, after-work meditation groups for professionals, parent and toddler groups, break dancers, cricket teams, book clubs, summer festivals, and music concerts – whatever connects with and expresses the particular context of a community.

Of course, the parish has inherent weaknesses and is not an immutable part of the British landscape. Particularly in urban and suburban environments, parishes need the flexibility to be porous, recognizing that many people make connections through various networks and gather from across parish boundaries, in gyms, cafés, church halls and so on.

---

47 Cited in Bayes and Sledge, *Mission-Shaped Parish*, p. ix.
48 Bretherton, 'Beyond the Emerging Church?', p. 42.
49 Grace Davie, *Religion in Britain Since 1945: Believing Without Belonging*, Oxford: Blackwell, 1994, p. 108.

Conclusion

The Christian faith is never transmitted in a culture-free or culture-neutral cocoon: it needs to be incarnated in the heart of each culture. Incarnating the gospel involves a careful attentiveness to the local culture. It involves communicating with people, as on the day of Pentecost, so that they can hear 'in our own tongues' (Acts 2.11). Attention to language, level of education, social dynamics, cultural idiosyncrasies, and the history of the parish is essential. These are some of the dynamics of inculturation. It is a process that is untidy and messy, mistakes are made, it is difficult in practice and takes much skill, commitment and time. Yet a generous ecclesiology means being open to seeing the Holy Spirit working in new, perhaps unexpected, places and people.

An essential dimension of Anglican ecclesiology is that it is communal by its nature. A metaphor that has often been used to express this corporate dimension is that of an ecclesial ship on its journey to God. An open, generous and hospitable Church has the advantage of being accessible and welcoming to those who are on a journey with faith that is 'limited and unarticulated',[50] with space for doubters, agnostics, the mentally disabled as well as the deeply committed:

> We are called to take the gospel to the whole culture, and that includes not only sailing to the other islands in the sea, but back to the mainland that we have left behind. We must return under the old banner of the cross, but this time we will not come to conquer but to sojourn.[51]

---

50 *Common Worship*, 1998, p. 200.

51 Andrew Walker, '20/20 Visions: The Future of Christianity in Britain', in Haddon Willmer (ed.), *2020: Futures of Christianity in Britain*, London: SPCK, 1992, p. 63.

4

On Popular Culture:
To its Religious Despisers

BRUTUS GREEN

It will perhaps surprise the reader of this day and age to find someone giving any thought to, let alone defending, the variously described, lewd, consumerist, vacuous, brutish or exploitative, institutions and forms of popular culture. Even more then will the eyebrow be raised at an attempt to convince of its worth such cultivated persons as those who declare themselves traditional catholics and utterly opposed to the lamentable secular nihilism of postmodernity. My suspicion, however, is that behind the pugilistic rhetoric, which rightly seethes at some popular excesses, lies a recognition of the fluidity of human life that requires the Church to be 'forever building, for it is forever decaying within and attacked from without'.[1] Given the longstanding creativity and spirituality of the Anglican catholic tradition, I shall appeal to these resolute defenders of the faith to look again for the unexpected signs of the kingdom of God within the grosser profanities of the world. Alongside this cultural generosity, I will argue that the Church is called to a more measured politics than the zealous anti-capitalism it so often voices. Such generosity may then be the basis for partnerships within the world in establishing God's kingdom, rather than a crusade against it, and a widening of how the Church perceives the company of the redeemed and approaches life and mission in the *saeculum*.

---

1 T. S. Eliot, 'Choruses from "The Rock"', II.

Secular and *Saeculum*

They say that ours is a secular age. Defined in terms of the privatization of faith, the decline of religious belief and practice, and a conception of religion as a matter of personal choice,[2] secularism is the enemy of faith and especially the established Church in its fighting retreat of Lords Spiritual, council prayers and religious symbols from the public realm.[3] In this conflict, *FTP* laments the marketing of the Church as a 'capitulation to the spirit of our age', finding it to be a 'contemporary milieu – by and large – to be vacuous, selfish and lost'.[4] The proper response is to take up counter-cultural arms: 'Christian difference is the basis of our appeal to a lost world, not studied similarity.' The Church bears witness through contradistinction, calling for the conversion of culture. The church building, as opposed to the Shard and other 'temples to Mammon' (*pace* the baroque splendour of St Paul's and the kings and queens of Westminster Abbey), is 'holy precisely because of its "otherness", which is not a sign of its irrelevance but a source of its true power... it challenges the values of secular power and secular idea of success. In that sense it is set apart.'[5]

On the other hand, we might recall the Augustinian definition of the '*saeculum*'. Avoiding 'Constantinian triumphalism' and 'Donatist separatism', Luke Bretherton reminds us that the *saeculum* of Augustine's two cities is 'open, ambivalent, and

---

2 Cf. C. Taylor, *The Secular Age*, London: Harvard University Press, 2007, pp. 2–3.

3 Further accounts of secularism are noted by Jeremy Morris in Chapter 2, note 8. Rowan Williams provides a useful discussion in his *Faith in the Public Square*, London: Bloomsbury, 2012.

4 *FTP*, pp. 83–4.

5 *FTP*, pp. 162–3. Davison argues towards a strongly fideist, almost watertight, approach to worldviews. His description of 'axioms', whether Christian, secular or other, as basic to reason and conviction (that faith 'is where reason begins rather than where it ends') suggests a very dim view of cross-cultural public conversation (Andrew Davison (ed.), *Imaginative Apologetics: Theology, Philosophy and the Catholic Tradition*, London: SCM Press, 2011, p. 14). See also Denys Turner's discussion of reason in relation to 'Radical Orthodoxy' theologians in *Faith, Reason and the Existence of God*, Cambridge: Cambridge University Press, 2004, pp. 94–8.

undetermined ... a singular reality or realm, ruled by Christ'.[6] The importance of this cannot be overstated. For the Church to set itself institutionally against the world is either to seek to gain power over it, to retreat defensively or to cut itself off from it. Ontologizing the secular as a force of anti-Christ or an inverted Jerusalem is misguided. The plurality of the *saeculum* is something to be negotiated; neither a neutral ground nor a battlefield, but two inextricable coterminous cities existing within a pluralistic society – a shared, ambivalent Babylon.[7] As A. M. Ramsey reminded us, the 'other city' is not to be identified with the Church, but rather where 'the power of divine grace and goodness is at work – in the Church, beyond the Church's visible boundaries and in the world-to-come'.[8] The Church is an institution of the *saeculum*, and the City of God, despite the perceived widening gyre, remains present to the world of secular institutions.

The temptation towards radical opposition underlies much catholic theology today. Rather than yearning for a golden age of Christendom, however, whether in pre-modernity or the Oxford Movement, the Church should be paying attention to how technologies are transforming human life and communication. Marshall McLuhan's comment that profound cultural change driven by media causes widespread anxiety and despair, and his claim that every sphere of life is continually being transformed by technology, remains evidently pertinent.[9] The

---

6 Luke Bretherton, *Christianity and Contemporary Politics*, Chichester: Wiley Blackwell, 2010, pp. 81–2.

7 '[A] missiological orientation implies neither withdrawal nor subcultural resistance but ... entails combining active investment in Babylon's wellbeing with faithful particularity and obedience to God' (Bretherton, *Christianity and Contemporary Politics*, p. 6 [cf. Augustine, *City of God* XIX, 26]). Rowan Williams's differentiation of 'programmatic' and 'procedural' secularism is helpful here (*Faith in the Public Square*, pp. 2–3, 19–22). There are undoubtedly programmatic voices that need challenging, but it is equally polemical for the Church to narrow the conversation to controversial positions: 'if we thought that the opposite of secularism was theocracy, we would actually be admitting the victory of secularism in the political sphere' (p. 19).

8 A. M. Ramsay, *Sacred and Secular*, London: Longmans, 1965, p. 15.

9 'All media work us over completely. They are so pervasive in their personal, political, economic, aesthetic, psychological, moral, ethical, and social consequences that they leave no part of us untouched, unaffected, unaltered.

Church cannot simply ignore technological innovation. The very attempt would ensure irrelevance. Romantic conservatism, however, arises from the beginning of *FTP*, where the authors argue that 'translation is treason'.[10] What they overlook is that in the rapidly shifting modes of the *saeculum*, every practice of theology, every liturgical expression, is an interpretation, a translation. And while they are correct that every translation implies a loss, it is also an opportunity for gain because translation demands re-creation. As the Reformation and Counter-Reformation demonstrated, times of upheaval in the Church's history match very evident losses with unprecedented cultural and spiritual creativity. If technology serves to facilitate communication, then equally, under the right conditions, it may facilitate the proclamation of the gospel and worship of the people of God.

How, then, should the Church translate its liturgy and forms of life in contemporary society? If *FTP* refuses translation and *MSC* is felt to play rather fast and loose with traditional accounts of ecclesiology and liturgy, how are we to make sense of the idea of cultural translation? Walter Benjamin's account of translation of poetry is helpful here. Translation is not simply transmitting information, he argues, nor does it stand on likeness. The point is not merely to find synonyms for outdated words, to change 'thee's to 'you's, to inject political correctness into texts or pander to current ideas of 'relevance' or short attention spans.[11] Benjamin sees that translations proceed from the 'afterlife' of the original: 'their translation marks their stage of continued life'; calling them an 'afterlife' because it is a 'transformation and a renewal of something living – the original undergoes a change'.[12]

The medium is the massage' (Marshall McLuhan, *The Medium is the Massage*, London: Penguin, 2008, p. 26).

10 *FTP*, pp. 7–8. Again this appears as the attempt to drive strong partitions between related, overlapping fields (in this case languages).

11 *FTP*, p. 74. Note, for example, Catherine Pickstock's shrewd analysis of the dangers of liturgical translation in 'Asyndeton: Syntax and Insanity. A Study of the Revision of the Nicene Creed', in G. Ward (ed.), *The Postmodern God*, Oxford: Blackwell, 1997, pp. 297–317; and 'The Confession', *Theology*, vol. 99.793 (1997), pp. 25–35.

12 Walter Benjamin, 'The Task of the Translator', in *Illuminations*, New

Benjamin uses metaphysical categories to explain the task of translation: languages supplement one another by their intention, aspiring to the 'pure language' hidden within them, and 'it is translation which catches fire on the eternal life of the works and the perpetual renewal of language. Translation keeps putting the hallowed growth of languages to the test: How far removed is their hidden meaning from revelation?'[13] Content and form can never be exactly reproduced but proper reinvention can recover meaning, which is forever dissolving. Translation is a yearning for this pure language. While in translations of poetry there is often thought to be a tension between fidelity and freedom, Benjamin's account of translation refuses this divorce by relating them both to the pure language, defined as 'expressionless and creative Word'.[14] Translation is not just modernizing; but neither is it an inspired work in the new language. The translator 'must expand and deepen his language by means of the foreign language'; it must be 'powerfully affected by the foreign tongue'. There must be creativity and continuity. The task of the liturgist then is to continue the afterlife of the Church's worship, allowing the evolving cultural milieu in which we find ourselves to be powerfully affected by the inheritance of the Church's worship and witness to the world. This also speaks to the larger act of cultural translation occupying the Church. We are at a point of cultural transition where prevailing modes of communication and ways of life have significantly altered. What is needed is for the Church to remain 'powerfully affected by the foreign tongue' and led by the Spirit. This perceived tension – rather, this dynamic of generous faithfulness – is the source of creative energy that should lead the Church's mission and sense of what it is about.

York: Schocken Books, 1968, pp. 69–82 (71, 73). Davison and Milbank repeatedly critique Fresh Expressions on the grounds that they will become quickly outmoded and dated. This is of course to misunderstand Fresh Expressions, which are intended to occupy specific moments; even in poetry, Benjamin notes, 'What sounded fresh once may sound hackneyed later; what was once current may someday sound quaint' (p. 73).

13 Benjamin, 'The Task', pp. 74–5.
14 Benjamin, 'The Task', pp. 80–1.

The mistaken conservatism in *FTP* is demonstrated in its assimilative reading of Pentecost:

> Pentecost means that this language is also common; we have diversity in unity. (It is telling that *Mission-shaped Church* misreads the speaking in many languages in Acts as 'translations' into multiplicity of cultures (p. 89), whereas the whole force of the story is to stress the undoing of Babel and the unity of the new disciples, who come to baptism that day.) There is no room in our conception of mission for an ecclesial apartheid, such as is expressed in the phrase 'mixed-economy church'.[15]

Babel is not undone by Pentecost, however; just as Christianity does not define its eschatology as a return to Eden. The utopian pure language of Zephaniah remains just out of reach in the *saeculum* and the welcoming of plurality – including that of a 'mixed-economy church' – is less 'ecclesial apartheid' and more the reception of the gifts of the Spirit. The proper preface for Whitsunday in the Book of Common Prayer celebrates 'the gift of divers languages', as the gift of the Spirit by which the apostles are to preach the gospel to all nations. Timothy Rosendale reminds us that, '[t]he Prayerbook had its debut on this auspicious day [Pentecost] in 1549, and this service announces a self-authorizing new enhancement through the vernacular of both the English nation and the English individual'.[16] The 'divers languages' of Pentecost are taken as the authoritative justification of the foundation of Protestant churches, including the Church of England. Even if we await an eschatological pure speech, it will be a new language tongued with fire; Christians do not look back to the garden of their past but await the new city of God's future.

If a first questionable tactic of catholic theology today is the polarizing of Church and world, here we have a second: beneath the sheep's clothing of desire for unity, a wolfish ex-

---

15 *FTP*, p. 142. One might particularly ask how appropriate their use of the word 'apartheid' is here given the seriousness of its history.

16 Timothy Rosendale, *Liturgy and Literature in the Making of Protestant England*, Cambridge: Cambridge University Press, 2007, p. 87.

clusiveness. This is best illustrated by *FTP*'s insistence on the definite article in 'the Church' and 'the faith', described as 'a preference for an idea over an actuality, for the virtual over the particular'.[17] 'Church' is criticized as 'vague', 'less historical', 'abstract' and 'subjective'. But do we really want cemented ecclesial boundaries? Are these not things we should struggle with?[18] The submissive attitude to the creeds, rightly questioned by Andrew Shanks for example,[19] is backed up by an authoritarian model in which the kingdom and the Church are collapsed.[20] 'Salvation is corporate and "Church-shaped" ... In the Church, salvation is displayed for the entire world to see.'[21] One does not expect to find the doctrine of *nulla salus extra ecclesiam* in the Anglican Church of all places, and yet *FTP* allows unequivocal statements of this: 'Salvation is a matter of incorporation into Christ through incorporation into the Church, which is his body.'[22] But which church? Determined by what boundaries? Perhaps 'Church' is less concrete and objective than 'the Church', with all the impression of a magisterium or subcultural haven that that gives; but if churches find their continuity more through family resemblances than an essential core, might we not be better off having a more open, versatile and, above all, generous sense of how Christ's body might extend in the world?

---

17 *FTP*, p. 113.

18 *FTP* footnotes Steven Croft's struggle with ecclesiological definition, deriding it as 'weak on ecclesiology', but the task of reimagining the Church is not straightforward – there is an ecumenical minefield to be negotiated, there are questions about the relationship between sacramental participation, faith, belief and practice. Not least there is a threat of presumption about an exclusive relationship between God and the Church, which leaves the world in the cold.

19 See his *Faith in Honesty*, Aldershot: Ashgate, 2005.

20 They rightly warn against the separation of Church and kingdom, but their anger at the neglect of the Church appears to blow apart a middle ground in which the kingdom of God is mediated in ways that include and exceed the activity of the Church.

21 *FTP*, pp. 44–6. Following John Milbank: 'The Church itself, as the realized heavenly city, is the telos of the salvific process', *Theology and Social Theory*, Oxford: Blackwell, 1991, p. 403.

22 Don Mackinnon, complaining of the 'deadly evils' of 1940s Anglo-Catholicism, writes of the 'temper of exclusion [that] encourages men to think of membership of Christ's Body after the manner of the claim *civis Romanus sum*' (*The Stripping of the Altars*, Bungay: Fontana, 1969, p. 25).

For *FTP*, it is Fresh Expressions 'that builds walls up' and their 'homogenous congregations are inadequate as gatherings of Christians, [just as] they are inadequate as communities into which to gather those currently outside the Church'.[23] Deploying boundary markers and contra-defining binaries of Church and world to the exclusion of many is equally a feature of this theology. The cultural translations that the Church has to make must not be defined by subcultural retreat and fear of the new. What is required is the re-creation of liturgical and ecclesial forms of life that continue the afterlife of the Church. If diversity is a feature of the *saeculum*, then we should continue to look for the manifestation of spiritual gifts which, beyond the grasping control of our instincts and institutions, reveal the transcendent God of love in new and marvellous ways. We must regard with suspicion the themes of radical opposition and exclusiveness that ensnare contemporary catholic discourse. We must recall the Church to a spirit of inclusive generosity. With this in mind let us now turn to the disdained contemporary world in order to inquire whether a less caustic approach might elucidate the movement of the kingdom of heaven in the world in which we live.

Modern Life Is Rubbish

> [W]e are hostile to the cultural condition of postmodernity ... [we] lament the current moral, cultural and economic climate ... the condition of postmodernity is largely something deplorable. It is shallow, callous, selfish and hollow.[24]

These are damning words. But they are also a strange thing to say, especially given the long association of Anglo-Catholicism and the arts. After all there will always be art, literature and music that will fail to resonate with an individual, community or subculture. With the aid of hindsight, we can look back to especially fertile periods of human imagination; we can also repent of the colonialism, exploitation and the silencing of

23 *FTP*, p. 66.
24 *FTP*, p. 117.

various minorities on which our past culture is founded; but can we at this very moment write off our culture altogether? Declare the time unpropitious? Amid a period of great technological development, which allows for undreamt-of possibilities across a whole range of media, providing far-reaching, immediate access to art, music and film for many in unprecedented ways, pronounce it spiritually moribund?[25]

The novelist Jeanette Winterson can fairly be described as postmodern. She is playful with truth: 'I'm telling you stories. Trust me.'[26] Her novels are riddled with non-linear, dreamlike, disruptive tangents, such as are associated with magic realism. Subjective experience is foregrounded at the expense of empiricism; we have *petit récit* not a grand narrative.[27] The epigraphs to *Sexing the Cherry* question the reality of both time and matter, and throughout her writing there is a typically postmodern preoccupation with power and a concerted effort to retell and subvert foundational stories including the Bible, fairy tales, Shakespeare and classical myth. She frequently embraces parody, but by and large criticism has preferred the postmodern denominator 'pastiche' to describe her work.[28] But while she has been associated with Derrida's refusal of exter-

---

25 For those who would argue such a position is only true for the elite sections of the wealthiest nations, one might consider Robert Jensen's and Emily Oster's paper 'The Power of TV: Cable Television and Women's Status in India', Cambridge, MA: National Bureau of Economic Research, 2007 (available at: www.nber.org/papers/w13305), which concludes: 'the introduction of cable television reduces son preference, fertility, and the reported acceptability of beating, and increases women's autonomy and female school enrollment' (p. 27). Cable television is rarely thought of as an introduction to high culture, but in a society that suffers from a frequently callous and deplorable attitude to women, cable television may have a role to play (cf. Steven Levitt and Stephen Dubner, *Super-Freakonomics*, London: Penguin, 2009, pp. 3–8).

26 Jeanette Winterson, *The Passion*, London: Vintage, 2001, pp. 13, 40, 160.

27 Jean-François Lyotard, *The Postmodern Condition*, Manchester: Manchester University Press, 1984, p. 60: the *petit récit* is the 'quintessential form of imaginative invention'.

28 Laurel Bollinger, 'Models of Female Loyalty: The Biblical Ruth in Jeanette Winterson's Oranges are Not the Only Fruit', *Tulsa Studies in Women's Literature*, vol. 13.2 (1994), pp. 363–80 (376–7); Tess Cosslett, 'Intertextuality in Oranges are Not the Only Fruit: The Bible, Malory and Jane Eyre', in Helena Grice and Tim Woods (eds), *'I'm Telling You Stories': Jeanette Winterson and the Politics of Reading*, Amsterdam: Rodopi, 1998, pp. 15–28 (26).

iority to the text and Foucault's rejection of metaphysics,[29] her writing is undergirded by a consistent realism. We find in the retelling of myths 'permanent truths about human nature',[30] most especially an investigation into the complexities of human experiences of love.

Her description of the writer's task in many ways reflects the same task of the philosopher that Don MacKinnon identifies in *The Problem of Metaphysics*: that of pushing against the boundaries of the transcendent. MacKinnon's work sketches the metaphysical potential of art, in which the elements of creativity and discovery struggle together to 'attempt the utterance of the unutterable', as a response to 'what is there'.[31] Cézanne is MacKinnon's primary example as an artist with 'a preoccupation with the transcendent',[32] exemplified by his valuing of tradition, mastery of technique, 'intense concentration of attention', a close relation of 'awareness' and 'imagination', all to the end of approaching simply what is there. But it is this paradoxical meeting of invention and discovery that is required for transcendence: 'he invokes resources of imagination, of spontaneously initiated constructive organization, in order to convey to himself and to realize in his painting the actuality that is in front of him'. Cézanne, for the empiricist, is a scandal, but for MacKinnon the paintings 'deepen his very concept of experience'.

---

29 Bente Gade, 'Multiple Selves and Grafted Agents: A Postmodernist Reading of Sexing the Cherry', in Helen Bergtson (ed.), *Sponsored by Demons: The Art of Jeanette Winterson*, Odense, Denmark: Scholars Press, 1999, p. 28.

30 Jeanette Winterson, *Weight*, Edinburgh: Canongate, 2005, p. xvi.

31 Pages 163, 154. Nicholas Lash later takes up this theme, arguing that 'in the relationship between "finding" and "fashioning" ... narrative forms are not the least important of the modes of discourse that we employ in our attempts to "discover"' ('Ideology, Metaphor, and Analogy', in S. Hauerwas and L. Gregory Jones (eds), *Why Narrative? Readings in Narrative Theology*, Grand Rapids, MI: William B. Eerdmans, 1989, pp. 115–23 (115)).

32 Don MacKinnon, *The Problem of Metaphysics*, Cambridge: Cambridge University Press, 1974, p. 106. For MacKinnon's discussion of Cézanne, quotations from which follow, see pages 104–13. Iris Murdoch, in *The Sovereignty of Good* (London: Routledge, 1970), also employs Cézanne for this purpose, primarily focusing upon his attention, quoting Rilke: 'He did not paint "I like it", he painted "There it is"' (p. 59).

But MacKinnon goes further in noticing that it is not merely the bland empiricist who may be rescued by Cezanne's attention to the concrete particular, who may be taught to look again; the philosopher may also suffer a similar, or even worse, enslavement if too wedded to his own way of seeing the world. The Platonist, for example, may emphasize the one over the many giving too little attention to the concrete and familiar, conforming experience to the shape of an overarching metaphysical structure: too often we see what we expect to see. A preoccupation with the transcendent requires, in this sketch, concentration and attention to what is there in itself. This requires a further skill, which is a feature of great art. There must be an openness to surprise; to discover what is unexpected in what is familiar: 'we have to allow for experiences to overtake us that shatter our frames of reference'; or, as Picasso framed it: 'You have to wake people up. To revolutionize their way of identifying things. You've got to create images they won't accept. Make them foam at the mouth. Force them to understand that they're living in a pretty queer world. A world that's not reassuring. A world that's not what they think it is.'[33]

MacKinnon's analysis of Cézanne illuminates our exemplar postmodernist Jeanette Winterson. Her work, as much as any other, betrays this preoccupation with the transcendent. She describes art variously as her 'rod and staff', the 'burning bush', an 'act of faith', 'the clarity of the Word', 'sacramental', as 'a reality beyond now', as 'pushing at the boundaries we thought were fixed'.[34] Equally she maintains that she writes within a tradition, admitting that '[a] writer uninterested in her lineage is a writer who has no lineage' and that, 'I respect tradition, though I'm quite prepared to vandalize it'.[35] She has a 'moral sense',[36] and describes art's relationship with transcend-

---

33 André Malraux, *Picasso's Mask*, London: Macdonald & Jane's, 1976, p. 110.

34 Jeanette Winterson, *Art Objects*, London: Vintage, 1996, pp. 20, 66, 95, 122, 148, 116.

35 Winterson, *Art Objects*, p. 172; interview in the *Guardian*, 22 October 2005.

36 'Face to Face: A Conversation between Jeanette Winterson and Helen Barr', *The English Review*, vol. 2.1 (1991), pp. 30–3.

ence as flight, liberation and rebellion: 'a daily rebellion against the state of living death routinely called real life'. Like Simone Weil, she is a voice outside the straightforward definitions of the Church, but which, through attention, imagination and a concern with what is there, may deepen our concept of experience. And Weil might well have agreed with her claim that the Church is offered up 'as a sacrament of love when really it is an exercise of power'.[37] Does the Church let itself be surprised by such voices? Does it dare take the risk of having its frames of reference shattered? Rowan Williams has written of the decline of scriptural imagination, arguing that 'Christian language actually fails to transform the world's meaning because it neglects or trivializes or evades aspects of the human'.[38] The Church, he argues, must wait and listen until it possesses the imagination to cope with the seriousness of the world. But perhaps there is something in Mary Grey's claim that '[s]acramental hallowing [is] a task to which not the theologians, but poets, artists and musicians have been more faithful'.[39]

While it is not possible here to examine a novel in depth,[40] it is perhaps enough to show that MacKinnon's description of the artist preoccupied with transcendence, with the attempt to articulate what is unutterable and what is there, with imagination and rigorous organization, tradition, technique and attention, with an openness to surprise, all suggest the possibility of contemporary writing seeking transcendence. Winterson's novels are filled with mischievous parables, a form that by its engagement with subjective experience is well suited to the transformational power of transcendence and is a keystone of MacKinnon's discussion of transcendence.[41] And we

---

37 'Face to Face', p. 30.

38 Rowan D. Williams, 'Postmodern Theology and the Judgment of the World', in Frederick B. Burnham (ed.), *Postmodern Theology, Christian Faith in a Pluralist World*, New York: Harper & Row, 1989, pp. 92–112 (106).

39 Mary C. Grey, *Beyond the Dark Night: A Way Forward for the Church*, London: Cassell, 1997, p. 67.

40 For a theological study of Winterson's *The Passion*, see my 'In Between Sex and the Sacred: The Articulation of an Erotic Theology in Jeanette Winterson's The Passion', *Theology and Sexuality*, vol. 13.2 (2007), pp. 195–210.

41 See particularly chapters six and seven of MacKinnon's *The Problem of Metaphysics*: 'it is of the nature of the parabolic, not simply to disturb or break

should not be put off by the secularity of these parables – if they are engaged with what is there. Simone Weil in her remarkable essay, 'Forms of the Implicit Love of God', writes: 'Every true artist has had real, direct and immediate contact with the beauty of the world, contact which is of the nature of a sacrament. God has inspired every first-rate work of art, though its subject may be utterly and entirely secular.'[42] Weil here is unafraid to expand the traditional use of the word 'sacrament'. In a particular memorable passage she writes that '[t]he longing to love the beauty of the world in a human being is essentially the longing for the Incarnation'. Here then is a truly catholic theology, in which theological categories are seen to burn themselves into the ordinary experiences of the everyday world of the *saeculum*. Here we can understand Weil's refusal to enter the Church as there were so many things outside it she loved and could not give up, that, as created, must be loved by God. To reiterate, it would be a strange claim to make to say that transcendence is for the first time absent now from contemporary culture. The implicit forms of God's love are there to be discerned in contemporary culture, but it is in their nature to be unexpected.

But how much ground will we concede? *FTP* understandably takes the easier route in declaring that the seeds of life 'are not to be found in much so-called "popular" culture, which has become in many areas the cynical manipulation of markets by recording-companies'.[43] Again, however, this attitude takes a

---

the stale cake of long-ago baked moral custom, by pointing to unnoticed possibilities of well-doing, but to hint, or more than hint, at ways in which things fundamentally are' (p. 79). See also Frank Kermode, *The Genesis of Secrecy*, London: Harvard University Press, 1979, and his *Poetry, Narrative, History*, Oxford: Blackwell, 1990; James Champion, 'The Parable as an Ancient and Modern Form', *Literature and Theology*, vol. 3.1, pp. 16–39; and Dominic Crossan, *The Dark Interval*, Sonoma, CA: Eagle Books, 1988. Crossan writes: '[Parables] are stories which shatter the deep structure of our accepted world and thereby render clear and evident to us the relativity of story itself. They remove our defences and make us vulnerable to God. It is only in such experiences that God can touch us, and only in such moments does the kingdom of God arrive. My own term for this relationship is transcendence' (p. 100).

42 Simone Weil, *Waiting on God*, London: Routledge, 1951, pp. 81–142 (106).

43 *FTP*, p. 132. One might ask how familiar the authors are with contem-

rather naive view of the past, in not recognizing the impact of market forces upon the history of art, while also denouncing a sphere that draws exceptional creativity, huge resources and has considerable influence. It is finally to this hated territory of consumerism and commercialism that we now turn.

The Ethical Consumer

One should either be a work of art, or wear a work of art.

Oscar Wilde

In Michael Ramsey's Scott Holland Lectures, he speaks of the early Church possessing 'a double strain of world acceptance and world renunciation'.[44] There is too often, however, a pull, driven by ethical and theological desire, towards world-denial and utopianism. In the first section I suggested that the Church need not retreat from technological innovation, even as it transforms culture; in the second, I suggested that the Church need not reject contemporary culture, that God may be discovered here in beauty, truth, goodness and wisdom, including in areas outside comfortable ecclesial territory. This section will argue that the Church should not retreat from the public square, but engage more fully in political life. In each case, I wish to suggest, the attempt to drive a wedge between Church and world is unhelpful and will lead to insularism, missed signs of God's kingdom and an unnecessary limiting of the Church's afterlives.

In *FTP*, consumerism is a dirty word.[45] Its attitude is encapsulated in this observation of good practice: 'Leicester town-centre churches combined to organize a very imaginative garden beside the shopping centre, into which to invite shoppers to be

porary culture. Alison Milbank's disparagement of computer games for lack of depth ('Apologetics and the Imagination', in Davison (ed.), *Imaginative Apologetics*, p. 40) neglects the frankly incredible depth of narrative and complexity that contemporary games possess and the imaginative possibilities and ethical considerations they permit.

44 Ramsay, *Sacred and Secular*, p. 8.

45 Cf. pp. ix, 83, 101, 104, 132, 198.

still and peaceful. Clergy were on hand to pray in a space that was pure hospitality, and a different order of space from the commodified, commercial world.'[46]

Again the theme of absolute cultural difference rears its head, beckoning a retreat to the garden of purity. *MSC* perhaps goes too far in its identification with consumerism: 'In one sense there is no alternative to a consumer society. That is what we are, that is where we are and that is where we must be church and embody the gospel.'[47] There is, however, at least an acknowledgement of a cultural change that must be engaged with, that carries some benefits and redemptive qualities, and in which the Church and the kingdom of God can be found. Luke Bretherton suggests that the Christian tradition offers tools 'to reform desire within existing patterns of consumption [enabling] ordinary political actors to express neighbor love and pursue a just and generous global good'.[48] Capitalism and Christianity are not necessarily irreconcilable, he claims, advocating 'political consumerism', which acknowledges the consuming nature of humans but finds that their desires can be more or less attuned to issues of social justice. By the creation of cooperatives, boycotting corporations guilty of malpractice, Fair Trade initiatives and ethical investment schemes, 'political consumerism can be envisaged as a way of cultivating virtue'.[49] The devil may wear Prada or indeed Primark, but shopping can be virtuous. Churches here may find a practical role in inhabiting networks in which action for social justice can be advocated, especially through the high-speed social networks such as Twitter and Facebook that currently provide the primary medium by which political consumerism is effective, not to mention their wider role in recent democratic and protest movements.

As well as offering a reforming influence on its own terms, Bretherton argues that political consumerism also acts as a counter-movement in so far as 'it seeks to re-embed economic

---

46 *FTP*, p. 198.
47 *MSC*, p. 10.
48 Bretherton, *Christianity and Contemporary Politics*, p. 176.
49 Bretherton, *Christianity and Contemporary Politics*, p. 181.

relations within social relations', creating an 'institutional plurality that serves as a bulwark against the totalizing and liquefying thrust of modern forms of economic power by creating alternative patterns of socially and politically embedded economic relations'.[50] Is the Church ready to use its imagination to engage with the seriousness of the world, to help recall the city to its ethical responsibility? Isn't this to some degree what is being observed by *MSC* in 'churches arising out of community initiatives' and what Andrew Mawson so impressively pioneers with the expression 'social entrepreneurism'?[51] Bretherton writes that 'in pursuit of common goods, the congregation has to listen to and learn to love its neighbours' with the goal being a 'partnership for common action between Christianity and democratic citizenship'.[52] If the Church is too ready to assert itself over and against the world it may miss its vocation to serve, participate with, and transform it.

But let us be specific. Contemporary culture, we have heard, is deplorable; the cynical propaganda of the market. Who inhabits this more than the icon of post-millennial pop Lady Gaga?[53] Taunted by detractors as 'raunch-pop', with mannered shock affectations, meat dresses and cigarette sunglasses, here is the standard bearer of the vacuous banality of popular culture. And yet no one takes their ethical responsibilities more seriously. She tells us that she likes 'the idea of seeding something political into a sugary sweet dance song', claiming 'I don't want to be a celebrity, I want to make a difference'.[54] And, like Jeanette Winterson, she is aware of the transformative power of art, especially mediated through popular culture of which she is entirely unashamed: 'Art is a lie. You have to tell a lie that is so wonderful that your fans make it true.' At the

---

50 Bretherton, *Christianity and Contemporary Politics*, pp. 185, 187.

51 *MSC*, pp. 57ff; Andrew Mawson, *The Social Entrepreneur*, London: Atlantic Books, 2008.

52 Bretherton, *Christianity and Contemporary Politics*, p. 220.

53 It would doubtless be easier to defend popular culture with a more respectable figure like Bob Dylan; however, it is my intention to suggest that the kingdom of God is within the reach of even some of the most supposedly commercial and 'low-brow' forms of culture.

54 In Peter Robinson's interview with Lady Gaga for *Pop Justice*, 23 May 2011, and Simon Hattenstone's interview for the *Guardian*, 14 May 2011.

same time she counters, 'My art is my whole life', with perfect camp authenticity, simultaneously embodying self-conscious, constructed narcissism and kenotically emptying herself for her beloved fans.[55] Is there a possibility here for the mediation of the divine through the highly commercial and secular?

As it happens, Gaga is not antagonistic to Christianity: 'Don't say I hate institutionalized religion ... I do not, what I'm saying is that perhaps there is a way of opening more doors, rather than closing so many.'[56] And on these grounds she has fought tirelessly against homophobic attitudes and bullying. She has received a letter from the White House commending her for her work on behalf of abolishing 'Don't ask, don't tell' and has been outspoken on issues of civil rights, immigration and education.[57] With 33 million followers on Twitter and 55 million Facebook 'likes' it is a voice that carries.[58] And it is a voice that is unafraid to address religion: 'to say God makes no mistakes [from Lady Gaga's 'Born this Way'] takes the knife away from all those who are prejudiced and religious. And that's why I did it.'[59] Like Weil, Gaga believes that God can use the cast-offs and rejects. Here we find a connection with Andrew Shanks, writing that 'if the gospel is in our day to be liberated from church ideology, this will indeed be thanks, above all, to the collision between church tradition and the work of new movements like the campaign for gay liberation'.[60] Shanks advocates public conscience movements as rallies for the 'solidarity of the shaken', suggesting that their honesty is able 'to confront the theological tradition, and recall it to its proper origins'. Ramsey captured the heart of Gaga's theological significance, asking in his aforementioned lectures: 'Is it not a part of this mind not only to perceive divine truths which are utterly con-

---

55 Neil Strauss's interview for *Rolling Stone*, vol. 1108.9, 8–22 July 2010, and Hattie Collins's interview for *i-D*, pre-Fall 2010. Gaga has driven herself into bankruptcy multiple times through personal investments in her show, and famously never appears as anything but the full 'Lady Gaga'.

56 *Guardian*, 14 May 2011.

57 See Lisa Robinson's interview in *Vanity Fair*, vol. 617, January 2012.

58 As of January 2013.

59 *Pop Justice*, 23 May 2011.

60 Andrew Shanks, *The Other Calling*, Oxford: Blackwell, 2007, pp. 187, 202.

trary to the world but also to perceive within the world, even in its unpromising aspects, signs of the presence and action of God and traces of his laws?'[61]

The cultic following of Lady Gaga, with her 'little monsters' gathered from the marginalized, queer and fearful parts of society, is given through the music and performances a liturgy and hymnal of solidarity. Shanks asks for forms of liturgy that promote solidarity and conversation, and rightly asserts the Christian tradition's history and expertise at public liturgy,[62] but against him stands a reactionary orthodoxy, an ecclesiastical fundamentalism, that has, and still does, repeatedly punitively marginalize and shut down conversation. Perhaps the aesthetic mode that is most helpful here in undermining this ideological seriousness and recalling the Church to honesty is *Camp*, an aesthetic with which the catholic Church is not unfamiliar. 'The whole point of Camp is to dethrone the serious. Camp is playful, anti-serious ... One is drawn to Camp when one realizes that "sincerity" is not enough. Sincerity can be simple philistinism, intellectual narrowness.'[63] Lady Gaga, who is the embodiment of Susan Sontag's definition of Camp, uses this mode as a democratic aesthetic platform to engage practically in political debate, which has a proven effectiveness in the technocratic world of social media. Bretherton argues that churches have a place in the public square supporting governments, which 'require cultural and personal changes that [they] are not able to tackle alone'.[64] Currently, however, it is this ambivalent, commercial-consumer icon that is doing more to bring about social inclusion, acceptance and reform than the ambivalent, prevaricating Church. Popular music contains within it the prevalent spiritual yearnings of our culture. Lady Gaga's *Born This Way*, which is redolent with catholic imagery, is a call to arms for inclusion, but also a marvellous,

61 Ramsey, *Sacred and Secular*, p. 61. He charges that the Church ought 'to be learning from the secular world about the presence and activity of God within it' (p. 59).

62 Shanks, *Other Calling*, pp. 202–4.

63 'Notes on "Camp"', in Susan Sontag, *Against Interpretation*, London: Penguin, 2009, pp. 275–92 (288).

64 Bretherton, *Christianity and Contemporary Politics*, p. 34.

camp assault on the seriousness with which the Church wrestles with prejudice.

FTP's mean-spirited side comes out in its desire for the permanence of a world that has all but disappeared. Fresh Expressions are dismissed for being of a particular moment: 'nothing is as stale as a fad fifteen years on', and yet are also criticized as a 'flight from locality, temporality and particularity'.[65] The Church, however, needs to engage with the world where it is. If practices of confession, support and solidarity are offered by websites such as *XOJane*, then the Church needs to also look for the signs of the kingdom in these ambivalent secular spaces while remaining true to its gospel foundations. The potential for recognition, for listening – for engagement with what is going on in the world – is there, and the Church in the depth of its tradition, its liturgical expertise, community organization and spiritual discernment must learn confidence if it is to play a role in public life. This will not happen so long as the Church plays its safe game of radical opposition, while it builds walls out of an anxious demand for unity, while it clings to its 'good taste' and shallow anti-capitalism. All of these efforts are retreating actions of defence that betray a lack of confidence in the faithfulness of God, like Peter sinking beneath the turbulent waves of Galilee.

There will be some who dismiss this as 'correlational' and a watering down of Christianity. It is not necessary, though, to divorce Christ and culture through 'axiomatic' differences; to reduce dialogue to shouting over a wall. Nor am I suggesting withdrawal from the tradition, which has from the beginning sought a constructive relationship with movements in aesthetics and philosophy. The work of cross-cultural interpretation and technological adaptation is already written across Christ's global and historical body in myriad afterlives. Finally, I certainly have no wish to compromise the sovereignty of God. In widening our appreciation of where the activity and signs of God's kingdom may be in the world, we avoid that most depressing human instinct to place God where God can be controlled and found on our side. This sort of concern with

---

65 Pages 9, 105, 117.

the sovereignty of God is so much more often really a concern with the sovereignty of some church or theology. If the pressure of ecclesiastical politics and insecurity over identity causes our grip to tighten sometimes on the reins to move at a pace we are comfortable with, then perhaps it is time to hand them back. The strength of Schleiermacher's defence of religion against the cultured elite in his time was his stirring advocacy of the universal human intuition of the divine, without dismissing the claims of positive religion;[66] an enduring testament against the narrow-mindedness of churches and the rootlessness of atheism. His apology provided a way back to the truths of Christianity, regardless of its popular superstition and vulgarity. The door Schleiermacher opened swings both ways in the ambivalent *saeculum*, however, and perhaps now it is the time for the vulgarity of popular culture to breathe new life into our religion:

> Even while the finite wishes to intuit the universe, it strains against it, always seeking without finding and losing what it has found ... Every revelation is in vain. Everything is swallowed up by earthly sense, everything is carried away by the irreligious principle, and the deity makes ever new arrangements; through its power alone ever more splendid revelations issues from the womb of the old ... so that through them and by them we might learn to recognize the eternal being; and yet, the old lament is never lifted that we do not perceive what is of the spirit of God.[67]

And yet the spirit of God moves on ...

---

66 See David Klemm's 'Culture, Arts, and Religion', in J. Marina (ed.), *The Cambridge Companion to Friedrich Schleiermacher*, Cambridge: Cambridge University Press, 2005, pp. 251–68.

67 Friedrich Schleiermacher, *On Religion*, Cambridge: Cambridge University Press, 1996, p. 116.

5

Where is the Kingdom?

JULIE GITTOES

Introduction

> There's a wideness in God's mercy
> like the wideness of the sea;
> there's a kindness in his justice
> which is more than liberty.[1]

The words of the nineteenth-century hymn by F. W. Faber articulates the expansive liberty of divine justice and the kindly judgement given in response to earth's failings. The breadth of God's love and mercy exceeds the measures of our minds. In contrast, we zealously magnify his strictness or apply false limits of our own. Redemption, in Faber's words, is plentiful; grace is sufficient enough for thousands of worlds. The challenge lies in the call to a simple love – trusting God's word – in order that our lives might be filled with joy and gladness in Christ.

In practice, the call to simplicity in love is complex. Words about the scope of salvation and the plenteousness of God's grace are easy to sing; indeed, they offer us assurance and hope. However, they are profoundly challenging in theology and practice. The premise of a generous ecclesiology is rooted in a commitment to worship and mission; the Church is formed by attentiveness to God and engagement with the world. Yet the world is already the arena of God's activity. How do we

---

1 *Common Praise*, Norwich: Canterbury Press, 2000, 'There's a wideness in God's mercy', p. 698.

avoid imposing false limits of our own by conflating the ecclesial community with the kingdom of God?

In responding to *MSC*, *FTP* raises questions about the relationship between the ecclesial community and the kingdom of God. However, it risks limiting the scope of salvation to the Church by failing to reflect on the nature of divine activity in the world, or the vocation of the ecclesial community within it. It values the givenness of patterns of worship and tradition without recognizing that the Church is also formed by mission. On the other hand, *MSC* recognizes that the innovation and responsiveness demanded by mission are intrinsic to the Church's being. Yet as well as neglecting the patterns of worship that enable the Church to remain coherent and purposeful, there is the risk of reducing the kingdom to improved 'networks of religiosity'.[2]

Both books reflect the fact that the Church is more than a building, a priest and services; both want to say something about the Church as a community of faith and action.[3] Neither publication does justice to a vision of a transformed society. Where is the kingdom?

First Steps

The Church exists for the sake of God's kingdom. That is, for the fulfilment of God's purposes for human flourishing, which are disclosed in Scripture. In order to embody that, we must be attentive to God in worship: in word, sacrament, praise and prayer. These practices cultivate healing and holiness, generosity and forgiveness, which in turn affirm that 'there is a new world both promised and realized'.[4] Worship draws us into communion with God and enables us to glimpse a doxological vision of the kingdom, which we are called to celebrate and

---

2 Rowan Williams, 'Fresh Expressions, the Cross and the Kingdom', in I. Mobsby and G. Cray (eds), *Fresh Expressions and the Kingdom of God*, Norwich: Canterbury Press, 2012, p. 1.

3 R. Warren, *The Healthy Churches Handbook: A Process for Revitalizing your Church*, London: Church House Publishing, 2004, pp. 83–5.

4 Williams, 'Fresh Expressions', p. 10.

pursue as 'critics and remakers' of the world.[5] Active engagement with God's ways in the world is part of the ecclesial vocation: the body of Christ is called to be both a sign of the kingdom and also to cultivate the capacity to identify aspects of God's new creation in the unexpected. As such, the Church is called to walk in the world, just as Jesus walked the land.

In this chapter, I will investigate ecclesiology as something dynamic – moving through the world and responsive to God's Spirit within it. I will do this by engaging with Dan Hardy's conception of a Church called to walk carefully in the world. This 'wandering ecclesia' moves, in Hardy's words, beyond the sanctuary into daily actions, imitating Christ by walking in the Spirit.[6] Thus the boundary between Church and world is blurred. As we shall see, this does not empty the Church of its distinctive prophetic witness. Rather, it allows for a generous encounter with those seeking hope, blessing and forgiveness in the midst of contingencies of life from birth to death; in faithfulness and betrayal; in joy, doubt and sorrow. The encounters occur within the boundaries of sacred places, in the context of intentional mission and engagement with the community, and in multiple contexts of human discourse and exchange. Transformation occurs step by risky step.

Such encounters are shaped by the Church's understanding of the nature of God's love, revealed in Jesus. This demands attentiveness to the light: to the radiance of God in worship, and to that light refracted in the world. The moving forward in hope foreshadows the fulfilment of God's purposes at the *eschaton*. Yet, without rootedness in the Eucharist, this wandering, embodied ecclesia is cut off from the primal event that constitutes its calling as society. A Church formed by worship and mission witnesses to a God of salvation; it seeks a kingdom where creation flourishes in response to God's generous love.

In this chapter, I do not offer a blueprint ecclesiology; nor do I intend to set out an ideal model of Church immune to

---

5 Williams, 'Fresh Expressions', p. 10.

6 Dan Hardy, with D. F. Ford, D. Hardy Ford and P. Ochs, *Wording a Radiance: Parting Conversations on God and the Church*, London: SCM Press, 2010, p. 85.

criticism or unaffected by the world. What is offered is something more risky, fragile, attentive and incomplete. This is an
invitation to see ecclesiology as something dynamic as well as
embodied – moving through the world and witnessing to the
activity of the Spirit within it.

It is a Church that is open to the truth of God; informed
by its Scriptures, creeds and traditions; dynamic in its social
life and engagement with the world; a Church that lives in
anticipation of the fulfilment of God's kingdom, reaching out
towards it in the Spirit. A vision of a Church called to 'careful
walking' enables us to glimpse the possibilities of healing and
transformation.

A Band of Colour

Dan Hardy, as an Anglican priest and theologian, reflected extensively on the nature of the Church – its holiness, its
missionary being, its structures, its worship. I will focus on his
contribution to Anglican ecclesiology in *Finding the Church*. I
will also engage with *Wording a Radiance*, in which he deepens
our understanding of ecclesial life by grounding it in a eucharistic pneumatology. His writing is dynamic and prophetic;
his creative use of language is typical of the imaginative theological engagement found within Anglicanism. Like Andrewes,
Hooker, Hebert, Temple, Gore and Underhill, Hardy reflects
the Eucharist in relation to mission, proclamation and service. He considers the nature of God's involvement in human
life, and presents a vision of the Church and kingdom that is
prophetic and practical. While acknowledging the fragility of
the Church, he articulates its distinctive character in enacting
and embodying a form of social life that anticipates the kingdom. We hope for its fulfilment, while taking seriously our
own historical/social particularities.

Hardy's capacity to express a vision of Church embedded
in God's being, activity and purpose means worship and mission are fundamental. He asserts that the Church is not able to
'be' itself or embody God's purpose with/in the world without

doxological generation (worship constituted); not 'able to "be" itself without moving, both within itself and with others (mission constituted)'.[7] We should recover the breadth and depth of divine generosity. His focus on abiding and being sent in the light and love of God makes him a generative and challenging person to think with. Hardy's theological approach was thoroughly committed to the world as the sphere of divine action and to the distinctiveness of the Church's vocation. The latter is expressed in words from the introduction to *God's Ways in the World*: 'the truth and purposes of God are "refracted" – as it were spread like a band of colour – in other forms of life and thought; and the purpose of theology is to rediscover the dynamic of God's life and work in this "band of colour" and from it'.[8]

Within the fragile networks of social meaning – including marriage and government – the Church has a distinctive character: 'it finds the meaning of society in God and seeks to bring society into closer and closer approximation to the truth that also frees people to be fully themselves, that is to the truth of God'.[9] We are called to rediscover the dynamic of God's life and work in the vibrant oranges, hazy violets and smudgy greens. Part of the Church's vocation is to reflect on the way in which dimensions of human life, in the midst of ever-increasing social complexity, are drawn into their ultimate fulfilment by God. The Church and world are drawn together into the kingdom of God.

That process of promoting the fullness of human society, he describes in terms of both light and attraction.[10] The Church, with all its failings and its yearnings, has to learn how to persist in its task in the world – being caught up in 'the perfecting

---

7 Dan Hardy, *Finding the Church: The Dynamic Truth of Anglicanism*, London: SCM Press, 2001, p. 38.

8 Dan Hardy, *God's Ways in the World: Thinking and Practising Christian Faith*, Edinburgh: T & T Clark, 1996, p. x. I am indebted to Dan Hardy's concept of God's truth being refracted in the world, and his challenge to the theologian to work in and from that band of colour. I seek to extrapolate that out to the ecclesial task.

9 Hardy, *Finding*, p. 240.

10 Hardy, *Wording*, p. 45.

movement towards fullness of God's creation'.[11] Liturgy has a place in drawing people to the light, but the Church is also called to relate to the world. As such, missiology belongs to 'an ecclesiology of opening and embrace rather than conquest and triumph'.[12] This opens the way to healing and flourishing in the face of fragility for the sake of the kingdom. It is rooted in attentiveness to the intensity of divine light, modelled on the pattern of Jesus walking in the land and inspired by the Spirit.

Dynamics of Attraction

To begin with, I will consider some of the key concepts within Hardy's theology: *extensity* and *intensity*; *attraction* or *abduction* and *sociopoiesis*. These terms relate to the way in which our human lives are lived out in the world, our creaturely condition; our focus on God and his presence with us that re-orders our desires; the way in which we are drawn to God, generating and reshaping our relationships. Then I will examine the impact that such a theological framework has on our understanding of Church – as formed by its life of praise, by its eucharistic worship, but also with mission as part of its being. Such concepts also refresh our reflections on the nature of the kingdom of God.

To speak of 'extensity' is to name the way in which we, as human beings, get caught up in things; it refers to our spread-out-ness in the world. It is part of our created nature that we are sent forth. However, there is a risk inherent within the gift of creaturely freedom that in being drawn outward we are in danger of losing the sense of God's presence with us. The culture of which we are part can add to this extensity.[13] For example, the dynamics of capitalism and consumerism redirect our desires and overwhelm us with choice; we are continually drawn out of our selves, living increasingly dispersed lives. Intensity is God's self-movement of love towards the world

---

11 Hardy, *Wording*, p. 106.
12 Hardy, *Wording*, p. 78.
13 Hardy, *Wording*, p. 68.

– in creation, redemption, the perfection of human life in the world.[14] This intensity calls forth a response; it makes possible human social life in all its fullness; it enables a movement of love between people. As human beings, we are, however, primordially attracted to God; drawn to relate to the divine.

In *Wording a Radiance*, Hardy introduces another term to describe the quality and the dynamics of this attraction to God: drawing on Coleridge, he uses the term 'abduction'. It refers to 'the capacity of our reasoning to be drawn by light, enabling us to "see" more than perception allows'.[15] This sense of attraction, of being drawn beyond the self to God, being drawn to others throughout creation, is redemptive. It is bound up with the formation of right desires and the participation in God's ways. Abduction is a difficult concept to wrestle with because of its association with force. However, the Coleridgian sense adopted by Hardy identifies it as a capacity to turn away from self-absorption back to our attraction to God and others. This primordial attraction is cultivated in worship; it also shapes our understanding of mission for it involves generating ever expanding patterns of relating. It offers a vision of what the kingdom is: a pattern of generous human flourishing.

What then of *sociopoiesis*? This concept describes the energetics of attraction – that is, the generation and shaping of relationships in relation to the divine. It embraces all spheres of personal and social activity including politics, economics, love and ethics. At an individual level, our personhood is transformed; our appetites become desire for God and for the well-being of the other. At the level of the nation, global society and the Church, Hardy depicts this interweaving of God's ways in the world and our engagement in this transformed pattern of relating by means of a diagram. The Church and society are not independent or mutually exclusive – there are multiple sources and directions of influence; Hardy recognizes the way in which 'care for the other' draws on sacramental energy, and how 'tolerance of others' names the social consequences of cer-

---

14 Hardy, *Finding*, p. 34.
15 Hardy, *Wording*, p. 49.

tain laws.[16] Hardy suggests that the Church moves civilization through the words and actions of prophecy and priesthood towards the kingdom of God. The former speaks into and within civilization to call it to something better; the latter stands within civilization, relating it to that by which it is perfected.[17]

The diagrammatic depiction of such connections expresses something of the complexity and subtlety of the relationship between the Church, the world and kingdom of God. It is not a linear progression from one to the other. Rather, divinely infused reasoning discloses how the kingdom can be both served and realized.[18] It expresses the distinctiveness of the Church's vocation, while also connecting the world to the source of its life and light. It enables us to recognize where the kingdom breaks through – for example, in the vision of the NHS as an organization committed to care and healing which was celebrated in the opening ceremony of London 2012 by Danny Boyle. It affirms the common good of the kingdom, while challenging the Church and world to strive towards it.

The sacramental shaping of relationships in the light of the divine life is an important element of the process of transformation; it is seen in Hardy's early reflection on the nature of holiness. He writes that the holiness of God is relational and performative. Holiness and God are mutually defining: holiness is the attraction to God, which calls and moves people; it is beautiful, satisfying and humbling.[19] God is one whose being is directed to human life in the world; but there is resistance, fragmentation and opposition on the part of human beings.[20] Healing – like a refining fire – comes about through the cross of Christ. What Hardy describes in his later work as *sociopoiesis* emerges from his discussion of the way in which holiness is enacted in the world. The Church, in its practices of worship

---

16 Hardy, *Wording*, pp. 51–2.

17 Hardy, *Wording*, pp. 52–3.

18 A practical example of this was vividly witnessed in a lunchtime recital organized by the music therapist at a children's hospice and hosted by the parish church: creativity, loneliness, grief, delight, limitations, youth and frailty were held together.

19 Hardy, *Finding*, p. 12.

20 Hardy, *Finding*, p. 17.

and mission, is shaped in such a way that it witnesses to healing. It must take account of the kingdom realized in legislation
that expresses equality before God. However, the kingdom
also calls for a prophetic engagement with difference and the
hope of transformation, without defensiveness and fear. Again,
this is difficult. It demands patience and attentiveness, which
stretches our human capacity. The ecclesial challenge of this
is especially poignant as the Church of England wrestles with
how to listen for the Spirit in the midst of synodical govern-
ance. It means being attentive to the neighbour; waiting for
difference to become a gift.[21] It means walking, one step at a
time.

These ways 'reach beyond what is conventionally associated
with "religion" – but nevertheless, the holiness of God demands
the proper interaction between ecology, history and culture,
for example'.[22] Social institutions also play a key role in the
performance of holiness. Yet the law and civil society are only
'provisional approximations to the good' for 'every attempt to
guide, to enact justice, to embody mercy, and to punish and
forgive, must pass through the refining fire of God's justice in
order to partake of the unnamed qualities of holiness and to be
energized by it'.[23]

To that end, the worship of the Church has a pivotal place:
'facing the holiness of God, and performing it within human
social life, is the special provenance of worship'.[24] Hardy
alerts us to the dangers of treating worship as 'routine' or the
error of regarding it as a human attempt to 'ascend' to God.
Rather, in worship, we are placed in a situation where we are
moved forward by God's holiness towards the good, because
of God's 'formative, freeing and energizing attraction'.[25] Worship takes place within the context of human resistance and
fragmentation; we are proved, refined, lifted up by it; it is a
real anticipation of the kingdom of God. Worship is not cut off

21 I am indebted to Rachel Muers's reflections on 'Contrary Vocations and
Patience' in the light of the General Synod vote on 20 November 2012.
22 Hardy, *Finding*, p. 17.
23 Hardy, *Finding*, p. 19.
24 Hardy, *Finding*, p. 19.
25 Hardy, *Finding*, p. 20.

from the world, in all its complexity. Instead it is the refining fire of Christ in our own particular place. The Eucharist 'enacts the intrinsic connection of all these [that is social, political and economic actions] to the inner dynamic of God's holiness, which depends not on the efficacy of the dramatic action but on the efficacy of God's holiness in it'.[26] God's self-giving holiness forms us: it shapes our freedom and our ethical responsibilities.

Holiness: Worship and World

Hardy continually refuses to narrow the ways in which we see the impact of holiness. He is patiently attentive to God's ways in the world, yet also describes the demands and challenges posed by the Church's worship to the world within which we live. For example, how might worship enact holy trust, a trust that forms the basis of society? Within the dramatic enactment of the Eucharist, a holy society is formed; a truest form of society.[27] Relationships are transformed by the commitment; living in expectation of an encounter with God prepares us to undergo a process of refinement. Hardy describes this as being open to 'moral density', which entails interdependence and calls forth both sacrifice and holiness.[28] The Church's pattern of sacramental worship, in particular the Eucharist, shapes its common life in relation to the divine attractiveness and enables both human freedom and responsibility. Given Hardy's concern for God's ways in the world, and the distinctive character of the ecclesial body, how might worship impact upon our understanding of the Church's missionary identity and purpose?

Hardy affirms that the world is the 'arena of God's activity' where God's purposes are to be fulfilled, 'intersecting with

---

26 Hardy, *Finding*, p. 21.

27 This is a real challenge within the Church of England in the light of the November vote at General Synod with regard to women and the episcopate. Romans 12—14 provides a prophetic challenge, revealed also in the Eucharist, about mutual affection, theological conviction and engagement with difference; it includes the recognition of how language is used by both the strong and the weak, and the potential for transformation.

28 Hardy, *Finding*, p. 23.

fields of human activity'.[29] This echoes his early reflection on the task of the theologian to think with and from God's refracted light in the world. The divine purpose for the flourishing of the social self takes place through the agency of the Church, as well as being connected to the Trinitarian life. The movement towards fulfilment is dynamic. The sense of movement within the Church is something that gains momentum itself within *Wording a Radiance*. To argue that the ecclesial community has a role to play with and in the world is about fostering relationships of attraction rather than triumphalism. To take seriously the created order of the world in all its rich diversity while affirming the place of the Church as God's purposes are fulfilled does not idealize either form of social life. The dynamics of extensity and intensity, light and dark, fragmentation and attraction reflect this.

Hardy regards the Church's participation in this work as fundamental to its being: 'understood in their fullest sense, both Church and mission are the social means of incorporating all the dimensions of human life in the world in their comprehensive fulfilment by God'.[30] There is a breadth and depth to Hardy's understanding of mission, which is conveyed in the diagrammatic expression of *sociopoiesis* and abduction. In displaying the different ways people '*are raised* to flourishing as society', Hardy acknowledges the divinely infused reasoning at work in the world.[31] *Sociopoiesis* refers to the capacity 'for generating ever-expanding orders of relation', which Hardy applies not just to ecclesiology but to the whole of creation.[32] The Church's mission is to point beyond the inhibiting factors of self-absorption towards a recovery of attraction to God, and all others. Church and mission are inherently social because they are grounded in the life of the Trinity, which also brings vitality and direction. To speak of mission is to speak of God's work. The world is God's – and all elements of human life are drawn to his light, holiness and love. This makes the

---

29 Hardy, *Finding*, p. 24.
30 Hardy, *Finding*, p. 25.
31 Hardy, *Wording*, p. 51.
32 Hardy, *Wording*, p. 53.

Church and mission more, not less, important, for both are 'embedded in God's being, activity and purposes' and are the 'self-acknowledged ways God's purposes are embodied in everything else'.[33]

The scope of this work is immense. The vision is to seek the fulfilment of all features of life, in anticipation of the time when all things are re-created by the light of God: the perspective is eschatological, the purpose is 'to make it possible for the light of God to embrace and transform human life in all its dimensions'.[34] And the source of this vision and its fulfilment is doxological. Worship brings hope for social life because it is rooted in the Trinity. The traditional marks of the Church – unity, holiness, catholicity and apostolicity – are not possessions, but gifts given in worship. Such gifts are for the sake of the kingdom: in order that the vision of social life and responsibility may be extended to all nations. The doxological marks of a new or redeemed humanity unite praise of God with life in the world.

An Invitation to Careful Walking

The Church is embodied and dynamic. Hardy writes of the nascent biblical Church thus: the 'significance of this new community does not lie in itself, but in its movement'.[35] These themes emerge in a less systematic but profoundly inspiring way in *Wording a Radiance*. The book that Hardy dictated in the final months of his life reflects an ecclesiology that is not a doctrine or idea; but, to repeat his own words within *Finding the Church*, it is a 'practice of communality in faith and mission'. His thinking is creative – a sense of relationality and fragility remain; the Church lives by being shaped by the past, attentive to the present and in anticipation of the future.[36] The Church's movement into the world confers forgiveness and

---

33 Hardy, *Finding*, p. 25.
34 Hardy, *Finding*, p. 25.
35 Hardy, *Finding*, p. 28.
36 Hardy, *Finding*, p. 84.

reconciliation: gifts received, practices learnt, ways of being embodied. The Church walks in the world for the sake of the kingdom.

A Church called to careful walking is a Church that is itself shaped by the 'measures' of Scripture and Eucharist. To be measured by Scripture is a hopeful and generative part of earthly pilgrimage. Here Hardy takes the medical term 'granulation' and uses it to reflect the healing power of Scripture; enabling people and societies to regenerate from within: 'Scripture does not deliver its healing from outside the pilgrim, but by drawing out the capacity of attraction that lies deep within.'[37] There is no neat reversal, but a hopeful release into freedom. This is the essence of the resurrection.[38] Scripture reveals a vision of the kingdom, rather than a set of rules, but the 'showing of the end of the journey ... the most intimate relation with God, with all humans and all creation. It is Scripture ... that discloses the Kingdom and the fullness of God's purposes. Scripture as a whole measures the Church, but the all defining measure ... is the sacrament of the Eucharist.'[39]

Hardy describes the Eucharist as that which gathers all aspects of social meaning in the world into an event in which the full truth of God is made explicit. The extensity of our social life is confronted with divine intensity. It is an interval in the normally scattered life of the Church – an interval in which there is a dense laying of personal stories, the reality of social life along with the tradition of the Church. In the context of worship all those dimensions of human life in the world are caught up in the grace-filled anticipation of the kingdom. The reality of our embodied existence in the world is set on a trajectory towards the fulfilment of God's purposes. For Hardy, the Eucharist 'fosters relational abduction'; the desires of the pilgrim are reshaped in relation to the other and God. Hardy describes this as recovering the 'primordial attraction'. Trans-

---

37 Hardy, *Wording*, p. 64.

38 Rowan Williams, *Resurrection*, Harrisburg, PA: Morehouse, 1994, pp. 39–40. Peter's failure is transformed into a new vocation: the sharing of the gifts of mercy and hope.

39 Hardy, *Wording*, p. 65.

formation extends beyond the individual to others in the world; attracting each person inwardly to God.[40] This happens in particular places, moments in time and in face-to-face encounters.

This takes us back to Hardy's sense that there is not a linear movement from Jesus to the Church, and mission. Rather, Jesus himself embodies all that the Church is in its vocation.[41] An ecclesiology of walking: this is demanding and takes time. Hardy, having been on pilgrimage to the Holy Land prior to dictating *Wording a Radiance*, writes of all that obstructs and deflects our human attraction away from God. As he writes about Israeli–Palestinian relations, he meditates on the directness and simplicity of Jesus' walking/healing. There are no grand schemes or pronouncements; instead, the wondering Jesus offers deep care.

Hardy suggests the Church should 'learn what to do next through direct engagement with him who meets us where we are'.[42] As well as patience and waiting, there might be puzzlement and frustration.[43] These are not seen as distractions by Hardy; but rather as opportunities for redirecting our attention. We see patterns in the ordering of the world that we had not seen before; focusing on the divine light deepens our theological inquiry. This pattern of ecclesial life – of walking, person to person – is done in the hope of healing. Hardy calls this 'granulation', a healing from deep within. It is a medical term that Hardy learnt and adopted. David Ford describes how he uses it for the way the Spirit wells up in us; the way in which Scriptures work within us; for the wisdom glimpsed in nature.[44]

How can we tell if we are on that path of healing-walking? Hardy suggests that it is revealed when our theological inquiries open up integrity and joy; when we see light in the other; when others see in us a new pattern of life. Part of the Church's calling is to make connections by, for example, naming in

---

40 Hardy, *Wording*, pp. 70–1.

41 Hardy, *Wording*, p. 83.

42 Hardy, *Wording*, p. 84.

43 Rowan Williams addresses the generative nature of challenges and puzzlements in 'Trinity and Revelation', in *On Christian Theology*, Oxford: Blackwell, 2000.

44 David Ford, in Hardy, *Wording*, p. 119.

human creativity, social concern and sporting endeavour, the virtues and gifts of the Spirit we are called to embody.[45]

'The individual pilgrim shares in the Church's eucharistic communion [which] extends beyond the sanctuary into all the daily actions of its members', writes Hardy. In this the Church should 'imitate Jesus by walking around, embodying a presence on the actual land'.[46] Such careful walking is deeply attentive to the light of God reflected in the world; and to the brokenness as well as the joys of those particularities and contingencies. However, it is also ordered, measured and guided. There is no loss of structure. Scripture and Eucharist are the prime measures of the Church's life; but the Church is also moved forward, step by step by the Spirit. Walking leads to theological and practical thinking in response; it stimulates the imagination of the Church as it searches out new signs and patterns. Hardy cites Receptive Ecumenism and Scriptural Reasoning as examples of deep healing that promote dialogue between Church and civil society.

A Wandering Ecclesia

A moving ecclesiology is not something 'done', set out and completed; rather it is 'conducted', a work in progress. A 'wandering Church' trusts in the capacity of the divine to transform all humanity. Such a possibility has to be made real in the life of the Church, and in its missiological engagement with the world. For the Anglican Church 'to enact a moving ecclesiology is for it to allow its worldly architecture (both literally and figuratively) to be shaped and reshaped in response to where it finds itself and what it finds there'.[47] This is a demanding calling, but also a hopeful and generative one. It is reparative in its promotion of healing. It is attentive to the life of the Church

---

45 For example, in celebrating the gifts of creativity, patience and fortitude in art and athletics at the Legacy of Sport and Beyond Limitations exhibitions hosted by Guildford Cathedral in 2012.

46 Hardy, *Wording*, p. 85.

47 Hardy, *Wording*, p. 87.

with its history, present challenges, in openness to newness. It resists obstructions and seeks engagement – in relationship, care and witness. Moving demands dialogue; it celebrates love of God and neighbour; it is about hospitality in relationship. It is rooted in the light and love of God and world.

An ecclesiology understood as involving 'careful walking' in the world not only expresses the interrelationship between worship and mission, but also provokes us to think afresh about the kingdom of God. First, it takes time. And that's hard and painful. It may mean staying with a conversation longer than seems bearable – knowing that it will change us; trusting that recognition will be possible.[48] Conversation ceases to be about reciting an argument or articulating a position until the other agrees; rather, it means speaking out of conviction while anticipating a glimpse of the truth in the other. In reorientating ourselves towards the divine light (in terms of attraction) we find the capacity to turn outward from our own particular agenda. We come to see the other differently; in the light of God, we address each other without despising or condemning.[49] It is a two-way process that is rooted in structures and guided by the Spirit. It is perhaps in this that a peripatetic ecclesiology can bear with the broken middle and attend to the voices on the margins.

Careful walking demands attentiveness to God and to the world. Hardy describes the body of Christ as 'those who have faith, love and hope for each other, and so embody God's work to reconstitute the social fabric of the world'.[50] Rather than being mutually exclusive, the life of the Church and the fabric of modern society are bound together relationally and with mutual influence. The Church is formed by its own polity: shaped by word and sacrament, the people of God are drawn into the purposes of God in learning the truth of others

48 Rowan Williams, *Dostoevsky: Language, Faith and Fiction*, London: Continuum, 2008, pp. 134–5. The dynamics of conversation and listening are complex and challenging: the refusal to cast the other beyond the scope of dialogue and recognition.

49 Being mindful of the language that the strong and weak use about the other is central to Romans 14.

50 Hardy, *Finding*, p. 91.

'through the deepest care for them'.[51] Alongside this the nation and global society are engaged in meeting basic needs and accepting responsibility for each other. To describe this in terms of abduction and sociopoiesis reveals that the movement and energy involved have their 'source in the divine life'.[52]

Each generation discerns how best to serve and contribute to the realization of the kingdom by this divinely inspired, or infused, reasoning. Pilgrimage becomes an 'opening of one's capacity to move indefinitely from self to others'.[53] An ecclesiology reflecting such careful walking is shaped by worship and embodied socially; it also both recognizes and strives for the manifestation of the kingdom in the world through participation in the complexity of its social life. It sees the fabric of the world as infused with divine light; it is caught up in the redemptive dynamics of abductive attraction. All this flows from God and is for the sake of the kingdom.

To recover a language of the Church as a pilgrim people raises questions about discipleship. To look forward to the fulfilment of God's kingdom entails a radical commitment to the world. We gather for worship; we engage in missionary activity. However, ecclesiology rooted in 'careful walking' places emphasis on the way in which the gifts of peace, assurance, forgiveness and compassion are embodied in diverse ways in the multiple encounters of the whole number of the baptized. It might be at the school gate, in the board room, at the supermarket checkout or at the football ground: all are occasions for face-to-face encounter and opportunities to name, embody or point towards the kingdom. Too often our discussion of discipleship focuses on service in the gathered life of the Church, or perhaps on close relationships or specific projects.

We do not cease to be the Church when we are offering legal advice or on duty as a classroom assistant. In those places we are still caught up in the energetic of attraction – seeking the flourishing of human beings. The experience of those exercising ministry as Self-Supporting priests and deacons highlights

---

51 Hardy, Wording, p. 51.
52 Hardy, Wording, p. 52.
53 Hardy, Wording, p. 54.

this tension. Too often their experience in the world of work or family life is not regarded as an appropriate source of pastoral or theological reflection; the expectation is that preaching, teaching and administering the sacraments (filling gaps on the rota) is their primary locus of activity. Rather theirs is a prophetic challenge to the Church and an inspiration to deepen discipleship; they work from the band of colour. The relationship between their vocation and the discipleship of the whole people of God echoes the imperative to imitate the apostles in walking in the way of Jesus.[54]

A wandering ecclesia offers a critique of the preoccupation with 'growth'. Sam Wells, in *Be Not Afraid*, reflects on how we confront or handle power within and beyond the Church. In the United States, the churches appear to have all the things we in the Church of England think we need (wealth, numbers, influence). Yet he goes on to note that 'it turns out that the kingdom of God is no closer'.[55] To walk carefully demands humility. When Paul addresses the Corinthian Church, he speaks to them of the light and glory of God; yet he also speaks of their fragility. They are to be ambassadors of reconciliation, not because they speak and act from a position of strength, but because they hold the treasure in earthen vessels. The light is defused in the world.

This pattern of careful, attentive, vulnerable walking enables healing. It might sound idealistic (especially given the way in which the Anglican Church has engaged with issues of sexuality and gender). Yet Hardy is not naive about this; his own experience within the Anglican Communion – especially of Primates Meetings – as well as his commitment to Scriptural Reasoning testifies to what a long, demanding and worthwhile process this is. It is difficult. It is time-consuming. However, it is only by improving the quality of our disagreements that we can deepen bonds of mutual trust and affection. It is right that we should be impatient for justice, and challenged by the world about equality before God. It is also right that this should be

---

54 For example, 2 Thessalonians 3.7–9; Hebrews 13.7.
55 Samuel Wells, *Be Not Afraid: Facing Fear with Faith*, Grand Rapids, MI: Brazos Press, 2011, p. 68.

balanced by patience to seek healing. Rather than getting stuck
with what seem like intransigent problems and differences, we
need to refocus on the glory and light of God and of the kingdom: 'it is not a matter of our working out every detail of how
to move on; we need to leave room for the Spirit to work'.[56]
A generous ecclesiology might take the risk of patiently working out how we live mercifully and gracefully with difference.
Not for our own sakes, but for the sake of the kingdom and
prophetic witness to a world that struggles with pain and
brokenness and the cost of our extensity.

A theology of careful walking celebrates the Church's calling as provisional. We live and worship and work between
the now and not yet. We are called to make real the divine
transformation. Yet the Church is also incomplete and fragile;
we continue to seek mercy in our own relationships, we work
out our disappointments and mistrust in the public sphere.
The Scriptures we read embody the complexity of human life
lived before God, and the struggles of holiness; the Eucharist
we participate in embodies brokenness and betrayal as well as
forgiveness and abundance. These practices shape us: 'As it refers all social meaning to the truth of God, the Church is much
more conditional than is recognized by those who suppose it
is somehow complete and perfect. Whatever grasp it has of the
truth of God, it still needs the deepest formation.'[57]

Sacramental practices allow space for honesty in failure and
brokenness while expressing hope, mercy and reconciliation.

When we become overly concerned with our own 'inner
meaning', we need to learn afresh how to persist with our task
in the world. The essentials of this are set out by Hardy:

Opening up the true potential and resources of human life.
Liturgy is one way of facilitating and helping people enter
into this creative dynamic and drawing them deeper into the
light, letting it penetrate and irradiate them. But this opening is certainly not exclusive to the Church: there are lots
of other ways, too, and we need to recognize and interpret

---

56 Hardy, *Wording*, p. 105.
57 Hardy, *Finding*, p. 241.

them in public life. It is about how the Church relates to the world.[58]

Examples of this are found in the spaciousness fostered in parish ministry: in birth, tragedy, celebration, grief and hope.[59]

Where is the Kingdom?

The nature of being the Church is embedded in the being, activity and purposes of a generous God. In the words of Faber's hymn, God's grace, mercy and love are abundant; the divine purposes in redemption embrace the whole world. Engagement with Dan Hardy's theology emphasizes the place of worship and mission as dual aspects of the Church's vocation, a vocation for the sake of the kingdom of God. The kingdom cannot be reduced to forms of ecclesial community in new networks or traditional patterns. The imposition of false limits undermines the relationship between the Church, the world and the kingdom. Rowan Williams expresses the generosity and intensity of the Church's life: '[it] takes cognizance of itself as a community which is open to all, which addresses God in total intimacy and trust, and which engages in mission ... Its vision is global ... Christian community has a focus for its identity in Jesus, yet the "limits" set by Jesus are as wide as the human race itself.'[60]

For Hardy, such attentiveness to God and world is expressed powerfully in the language of abduction, the radical re-ordering of relationships. Language of abduction is challenging, because it disrupts our understanding of autonomy. However, it enables the wandering ecclesia to be faithful, critical and responsive. The divine light addresses the extensity of our human existence. The Church lives in relation to the white light and

58 Hardy, *Wording*, p. 106.

59 *Praying for England* captures such examples. The challenge of the Occupy Movement and St Paul's raises questions of justice and equity at a national and global level; in Hampton, hosting a hospice carol service for siblings, parents and staff reflects a more local engagement with grief, hope and compassion.

60 Williams, 'Trinity and Revelation', p. 137.

the refracted band of colour; it gathers for worship and is dispersed in the world. To think of our ecclesiology as 'moving' acknowledges that the Church is a pilgrim people on the way. As the entire community of the baptized walk in the world, they are called to mediate the gift of renewed relationship. The concept of *sociopoiesis* expands our vision of God's kingdom and fosters imaginative engagement with the world.

Hardy describes the Eucharist as the gathered 'interval' in the scattered life of the Church. It is an interval in which we are 'measured' and 're-shaped'. Such patterns and practices enable attentiveness, stability and faithfulness. To walk in the world, to be a 'wandering' Church, is risky, gracious, challenging and transformative. There is no place for complacency, but instead a demand to engage in what Tim Jenkins calls 'an experiment in providence'.[61] Historically, Anglicanism has maintained a healthy engagement with the changing patterns of society, seeking to proclaim afresh the gospel, while also placing the Eucharist at the heart of both continuity and improvisation.

The Church cannot be itself or embody God's purpose in the world without being constituted by its worship; nor can the Church be itself without 'moving', without being constituted by mission.[62] To be a holy, catholic and apostolic Church is to be in communion with God, in community with one another and to engage in communication with the world.[63] This vision of Church and mission is sustained – despite all the practical problems and tensions that confront us – because the Church is the body of Christ. As such we are gathered and sent. The gift of assurance and healing deepens commitment to the world; it makes us alert to the kingdom breaking through here and now. The eschatological hope of fulfilment acts as a check and balance, guarding against conflating the kingdom with the Church or identifying it uncritically with the world.

The Church is rooted in Jesus' ministry; it is rooted in the generosity of God in creation; it is rooted in the life of the Spirit.

61 T. Jenkins, *An Experiment in Providence: How Faith Engages the World*, London: SPCK, 2006, p. 8.

62 Hardy, *Finding*, p. 40.

63 Stephen Cottrell, *From the Abundance of the Heart*, London: Darton, Longman & Todd, 2006, p. 12.

The Church witnesses, proclaims, and walks. Transformation occurs in encounter with God and the other, as the body of Christ walks in the world. It is a creative, demanding and joyful vocation for the sake of the kingdom. We need:

> healthy complexity in which local churches exemplify a sensitivity to the special needs of people while knitting them into a dynamic society both local and worldwide. Much of this will be achieved through small – and often risky – steps of generosity ... differences of people can be built into a dynamic society. And our vision of God should make these 'small confirmations' into a movement of exciting generosity and gladness.[64]

---

64 Hardy, *Finding*, p. 89.

6

A Strangely Warmed Heart in a Strange and Complex World: On Assurance and Generous Worldliness

TOM GREGGS

There is a strange and perhaps unexpected by-product of living in an age of what appears to be the rapid de-christianization of Western Europe, with projections about the disappearance of denominations and the terminal decline of the Church.[1] The unexpected by-product is: locating the Church with assurance has become an increasingly easy task. We are no longer as concerned about those who attend out of societal and cultural expectation, and congregations largely consist of those who wish to identify with the active community of faith. The increasingly counter-cultural nature of the decision to attend church both demarcates the Church and its members and makes the Church community a visible, identifiable and distinguishable one in contradistinction to the world. In the context of secularization and pluralism, the very continued existence of the Church has meant that it has come (over and

---

1 For example, the Right Reverend Paul Richardson in his article 'Britain is No Longer a Christian Nation', *Sunday Telegraph*, 27 June 2009, suggests the Church of England could disappear within a generation, given that the falling numbers in Sunday morning congregations is accelerating at around 1 per cent per annum, and on this basis it is difficult to see the Church surviving for more than 30 years. For more on church attendance figures and the situation in Europe, see Grace Davie, *Europe: The Exceptional Case: Parameters of Faith and the Modern World*, London: Darton, Longman & Todd, 2002, pp. 6–7, and her *Religion in Britain Since 1945*, London: Blackwell, 1994, pp. 46–9.

against prevailing cultures which 'believe' but do not 'belong' to an institutional form of Christianity)[2] in almost all forms to understand itself with some sense of the ecclesiology of the radical reformation:[3] there is a clear distinction to the rest of society. For those from more evangelical traditions, this identifiable confidence has expressed itself in terms of individualized personal salvation: in contrast to the rest of society, 'I' am saved. For those from more catholic traditions, this identifiable self-confidence has expressed itself communally in the locatedness of the visible Church: the Church's sacred space is clearly distinguishable (in its traditions, forms and practices) from secular space. In both cases, unhelpful (ungenerous) forms of ecclesial self-understanding and practice arise.

In this chapter, I wish – from a Methodist perspective – to reflect on the theological understanding of assurance that underlies such self-certainty, either in terms of a collection of individually assured believers or of the Church's form and practice. I will then reflect on the doctrine of assurance in relation to the expression of it by John Wesley during the Evangelical Revival of the eighteenth century, using this as a mode of repair to unhelpful contemporary understandings of assurance that underlie the current ecclesial setting. I will then apply this repaired understanding of assurance to ecclesiology to demonstrate how a properly understood doctrine of assurance has the potential to provide a basis for a more generous understanding of the Church that is more fitting to the gospel and more helpful for the contemporary cultural condition of post-Christendom.

Unhelpful Binaries and Confident Self-assurance

The contemporary situation of declining church attendance has rightly drawn attention from all kinds of ecclesial traditions. At times, decline has brought about (in the words of

---

2 See Davie, *Religion in Britain Since 1945*, chapter 6.

3 Cf. David Fergusson, *State, Church and Civil Society*, Cambridge: Cambridge University Press, 2004, p. 44.

Michael Jinkins) 'the hyperactivity of panic. This manifests it-self in clutching for any and every programmatic solution and structural reorganization in the desperate hope that survival is just another project or organizational chart away.'[4] Usually, survival concerns getting those 'outside' into the 'inside'; those who do not attend church to attend church; those who are not 'saved' to be saved; those who do not receive sacraments to receive sacraments; and so on. In other words, in response to the contemporary setting, the Church has presumed that it operates with clear identifiable binaries, and that the activity of the Church is to move people from one side of a binary, across a relatively clearly defined boundary, to the other side of the binary. In forms of piety that are associated with evangelical Protestantism, this binary is usually expressed as some form of the saved–damned distinction (believer or non-believer; Christian or non-Christian).[5] But even if expressed differently, such a distinction is found in other forms of piety and eccle-sial settings: secular–sacred, Church–world, and so on. What underlies such binaries is an assurance about who counts as 'us' and who counts as 'them', whether expressed in terms of per-sonal salvation or ecclesial identity. Although there might be considerations around where the boundary lies, there is never-theless clarity that such a boundary exists and is relatively easy to spot: a little like an elephant, it may be difficult to describe, but you know where it is. Furthermore, and perhaps unexpect-edly, even in modes of church expression that are oriented on being 'culturally relevant', such a binary underscores missional practice and ecclesial identity. So, for example, *MSC* speaks of the transformed approach to mission in the following ways:

> church plants and fresh expressions of church represent the
> emergence of a diametrically different approach that is both

---

4 Michael Jinkins, *The Church Faces Death: Ecclesiology in a Post-Modern Context*, New York and Oxford: Oxford University Press, 1999, p. 9.

5 For more on binaries in relation to salvation, see my *Barth, Origen, and Universal Salvation: Restoring Particularity*, Oxford: Oxford University Press, 2009, especially preface and chapter 7. On binaries more generally, see Peter Ochs, *Pierce, Pragmatism and the Logic of Scripture*, Cambridge: Cambridge University Press, 1998, chapter 8.

theologically appropriate and strategically significant. Instead of 'come to *us*', this new approach is 'go to *them*'. We need to find expressions of church that communicate with *post-Christian people*, and which enable them to become committed followers of Jesus Christ. Then *they*, in turn, can continue to engage in mission with and beyond *their own culture*.[6]

This issue at stake is more profound for a generous ecclesiology than simply whether the Church is (or is best) expressed as a parish or gathered community or some other mode of community: the point is not geographical.[7] The issue at stake concerns more what the Church is, and how that nature determines the way the Church understands its relation to the *rest of* the world as part of the world itself.[8] Or, put otherwise: what is the Church assured of, and how does this determine its self-understanding and actions?

Current discussions of ecclesiology that focus so much on form, and that do so to be clear about (or to justify) where we might have assurance that the Church is, are in large part pre-occupied with the self: either the self of an individual believer or of the communal ego of the particular form of the Church (parish versus network, etc.). This issue of ecclesial/believers' self-understanding in relation to a society that identifies itself in large part as non-Christian (or at least non-practising) is obviously in certain ways a particularly modern problem: when societies were religiously homogenous, such issues were not as pronounced; previously the issue might have been *degree* of fervour, or *regularity* of participation, but not whether or not one belonged to the Church. Given that there are those in society who do not identify as believers or communicant church members, it is hardly surprising that the Church thinks of itself in distinction to those others. But care must be taken that those thought processes about the relation of the Church

---

6 *MSC*, p. 12, emphasis added.

7 Cf. the concerns in *MSC*, p. 7, over networks or parishes.

8 Note here that I do not speak in terms of Church–world, but in terms of Church (as part of the world)–rest of the world.

to *the rest of society* (of which the Church is also a part) use appropriate theological categories. Care must be taken that the assurance that underlies the discussions of church identity is an assurance that comes from the activity of God, and not an ill-found self-confidence. John Wesley's pronouncement (in characteristic eighteenth-century tones) sounds a warning that the contemporary Church would do well to heed: 'How many have mistaken the voice of their own imagination for this "witness of the Spirit" of God, and thence idly presumed they were the children of God while they were doing the work of the devil!'[9] Even if we might not wish to use the same language to express the point, the issue of self-deception and the importance of self-critical examination have much to say to a contemporary Church that argues over its form but is confident of its nature.

One way to overcome this problem would be (and perhaps has been) to lose all confidence in the Church altogether: to see the broken and created Church with all its propensity to sin and self-deception as entirely unredeemable; to see the feeling and assurance of salvation for the children of God as located in the human psyche; to see God as so objective and distant that the experience of salvation could have no appropriately theological grounds. Thus, perhaps, lies the road to the sort of deism that most people in Western Europe effectively practise.[10] But a community without any confidence could not be described in terms of a generous ecclesiology: it would have nothing to be generous with. Experience of God and assurance has always been part of faith: we need only to pray the Psalms to discover that; Scripture is full of descriptions of what it means to be the children of God.[11] The problem is not *whether* God allows Godself to be experienced in the life of the believer and the life of the Church. The problem is *how* we think about that experience and assurance. Wesley makes the point that a madman's imagining himself to be the king does not mean

---

9 Albert C. Oulter (ed.), *The Works of John Wesley*, Nashville: Abingdon Press, 1984, vol. 1 (henceforth *Sermons I*), p. 267.

10 Cf. Davie, *Religion in Britain Since 1945*, chapter 5, where Davie discusses people's belief in the 'ordinary god'.

11 *Sermons I*, p. 271.

that there are no kings.[12] Unhelpful ways of thinking about the assurance of being God's children do not mean that assurance is not offered to believers and the Church. The issue is what sort of assurance God offers to God's people, and how are we to understand that assurance. It is to this issue that this chapter now turns in examining John Wesley's account of assurance.

Re-examining Assurance

In the theology of John Wesley we find an account of assurance that helpfully cuts through many of the problematic features identified thus far with particular forms of assurance associated with contemporary expressions of pietism and evangelicalism in relation to the individual, and – perhaps indeed – contemporary forms of ecclesial assurance in more catholic traditions in relation to the whole Church. In Wesley's three sermons on assurance (Sermons 10–12), he recognizes problematic features of Christian assurance, and offers an account of assurance that is potentially fruitful for a generous ecclesiology. Three of Wesley's central points will be examined to identify a pneumatological, humble, world-oriented account of assurance that could have positive effects on ecclesial self-understanding in relation to the world.

Assurance is not self-assurance: the activity of the Spirit and the message of Scripture

For Wesley, it is very clear that the source of assurance is located in the activity of God the Holy Spirit and that this is known through the testimony of Holy Scripture.[13] Unlike accounts that locate assurance in humanity and in feelings,[14]

---

12 *Sermons I*, p. 293.

13 In identifying the economy of the Spirit as the locus for assurance, Wesley makes use of the doctrine of appropriations.

14 Cf. Friedrich Schleiermacher, *The Christian Faith*, Edinburgh: T & T Clark, 1968, pp. 12ff. Schleiermacher is concerned here with the feeling of 'absolute dependence', which he identifies as a feeling of being in relation to God.

Wesley sees (in terms of the order of being) assurance to be located in the activity of the Spirit of God, who is at work in believers. The account of human assurance is an account of the economy of God who works from outwith the believer within the believer: 'Since therefore the testimony of his [God's] Spirit must precede the love of God and all holiness, of consequence it must precede our consciousness thereof.'[15] This consciousness must be 'distinguished from the presumption of a natural mind'.[16] The joy of the assured Christian is not based upon any anthropological condition or cause: 'this is not a *natural* joy'.[17] Furthermore, in terms of the order of knowing in relation to this assurance, Wesley is clear that the reality that a believer can feel of the assurance of the Spirit is derived from the teaching of Scripture: the activity of the life of the Spirit in the believer is paid testimony to in Scripture, and thus the believer might be assured because she is taught in Scripture that the Spirit assures the believer. For Wesley, the experience of assurance is a reality not primarily because of the experience itself (which could be one of self-deception), but because the Bible teaches that the Spirit works within the hearts of the children of God.[18] The text for Sermons 10 and 11 is Romans 8.16: 'The Spirit itself beareth witness with our spirit that we are the children of God.' Since Scripture teaches this, Wesley asserts that it must be a reality for the believer today; and it is only in applying to oneself the marks of the children of God as described in the Bible that one might know if one is a child of God. Thus, writes Wesley, in Scripture: 'He that now loves God – that delights and rejoices in him with an humble joy, an holy delight, and an obedient love – is called a child of God; But I thus love, delight, and rejoice in God; Therefore I am a child of God; then a Christian can in no wise doubt of his being a child of God.'[19]

Both in terms of the order of being and in terms of the order of knowing, individual feeling and interiority is the *final* stage

---

15 *Sermons I*, p. 290.
16 *Sermons I*, p. 277 (cf. pp. 277ff.).
17 *Sermons I*, p. 310.
18 *Sermons I*, p. 271.
19 *Sermons I*, p. 276.

of assurance, and not the foundation of assurance: the activity of God, and knowledge of God's economy in Scripture, are foundational.[20] Indeed, Wesley identifies a stage *before* the inward assurance of being a child of God that is discernible in his above deduction – the active life of a child of God. For Wesley, exteriority is the first product of the life in which the Spirit acts, and which the Bible teaches is the life of a child of God: 'we must be holy of heart and holy in life *before* we can be conscious that we are so, before we can have "the testimony of our spirit" that we are inwardly and outwardly holy'.[21] The faithful are assured of being children of God only after they are holy of heart and in life. In Wesley, therefore, consciousness of being a child of God (assurance) follows from the activity of the Spirit in human lives; from the knowledge that God does this work, as it is taught in Scripture; and from the reality of lives that are being transformed into holiness. It is only after the latter, that one might become assured.

At this point, the question arises of what it is that Christians can be assured of, and how is it that they know that their assurance is the activity of the Spirit and not anthropological self-assurance, which is a deception. Here, Wesley offers an account based on repentance, and on the outward orientation of the believer and the fruits of the Spirit. It is to these that this chapter now turns.

The assurance of radical de-assurance: assured of the need to repent

For Wesley, the first identifying feature of assurance is in one sense the radical de-assurance that is found in the need for repentance. Assurance is not about a self-confident approach to

---

20 This is a point on which Wesley does not move (Sermons I, p. 287), despite the fact that he does shift from initially believing that assurance was necessary for salvation to believing, in his more mature thought, that it was not (cf. Colin W. Williams, *John Wesley's Theology Today*, London: Epworth Press, 1962, p. 112).

21 *Sermons I*, p. 274, emphasis added. This seems to differ from the order offered by Schleiermacher: feeling, for him, is distinguished from (and more primary than) doing. See Schleiermacher, *The Christian Faith*, pp. 5–12.

God and the gifts of God, nor is it a single momentary confirmation of one's salvation to carry one through life. Instead, the
first mark of assurance is the conviction of sin in the believer.[22]
In comparison to the 'presumptuous self-deceiver', the assured
believer is described by Wesley in the following terms:

> The Scriptures describe that joy in the Lord which accom-
> panies the witness of his Spirit as an humble joy, a joy that
> abases to the dust; that makes a pardoned sinner cry out, 'I
> am vile! ...' And wherever lowliness is, there is meekness,
> patience, gentleness, long-suffering. There is a soft, yielding
> spirit, a mildness and sweetness, a tenderness of soul which
> words cannot express. But do these fruits attend that *sup-
> posed* testimony of the Spirit in a presumptuous man? Just
> the reverse.[23]

The one who does not – in being conscious of God's presence
in her spirit – repent, but becomes confident of her assurance,
grows haughty in her behaviour. To her, Wesley proclaims:
'Discover thyself, thou poor self-deceiver! Thou who art confident of being a child of God ... O cry unto him, that the scales
may fall from thine eyes ...'[24] For Wesley, assurance comes not
after the act of repentance, but *in* the very act of repentance:
only in hearing the sentence of death do Christians hear the
voice of the one who says 'Your sins are forgiven'.[25] Further-

---

22 This is a point that is paralleled in the work of the nineteenth-century
German pietist Blumhardt. See Simeon Zahl, 'The Spirit and the Cross: Engaging
a Key Critique of Charismatic Pneumatology', in Jane Williams (ed.), *The Holy
Spirit and the World Today*, London: Alpha, 2011.

23 *Sermons I*, pp. 279–80. Cf. Luther: 'God receives none but those who are
forsaken, restores health to none but those who are sick, gives sight to none but
the blind, and life to one but the dead. He does not give saintliness to any but
sinners, nor wisdom to any but fools. In short: He has mercy on none but the
wretched and gives grace to none but those who are in disgrace. Therefore no
arrogant saint, or just or wise man can be material for God, neither can he do the
work of God, but he remains confined within his own work and makes of himself
a fictitious, ostensible, false, and deceitful saint, that is, a hypocrite.' Jaroslav
Pelikan and Daniel E. Poellot (eds), *Luther's Works*, vol. 14, St Louis: Concordia
Publishing House, 1958, p. 163.

24 *Sermons I*, p. 281.

25 Williams, *John Wesley's Theology Today*, p. 106.

more, for Wesley, this is far from a single moment or event: it is rather a continuous state of being. As Karl Barth points out, when we have to do with the Spirit, we have to do with the eschatological presence of God in the present: in St Paul's language, the Spirit is a 'guarantee' or 'deposit' (*arrabōn*) of a future reality. This reminds us that, in Barth's words, in the present, we 'believe in an eternal life even in the midst of the valley of death. In this way, in this futurity, we have it. The assurance with which we know this having is the assurance of faith, and the assurance of faith means concretely the assurance of hope.'[26] According to Wesley, therefore, we are wise to cry continually to God.[27] Assurance is a state of continual crying out to God in repentance, as opposed to a state of self-confidence in one's status based on some singular event.

Outwards orientation: assurance from loving the world and fruits of the Spirit

In contrast to understandings of assurance as focused upon the interiority of a believer, who is able to concentrate on her own personal salvation rather than be concerned with the communities and lives of those around her, Wesley's account of assurance is focused radically away from the self and towards others. For Wesley, beyond repentance, one's assurance comes from being 'saved from the pain of proud wrath'. In concrete terms, this is an orientation away from self and towards neighbour.[28] Indeed, this echoes Luther's assertion that those who lack assurance are in fact self-centred;[29] and Wesley states overtly that 'you must be directly assured if you love your neighbour as yourself; if you are kindly affectioned to all mankind, and full

---

26 Karl Barth, *Church Dogmatics* I.1, Edinburgh: T & T Clark, 1975, p. 463.

27 Cf. *Sermons I*, p. 298. Wesley makes the point here in relation to prevenient grace, but the point regarding continuation remains: indeed, the context of these remarks are within times of strong temptation when the fruits of the Spirit are 'clouded' (*Sermons I*, p. 297).

28 *Sermons I*, p. 273.

29 Cf. Gerhard Ebling, *Luther: An Introduction to His Thought*, London: Collins, 1970, pp. 37–8.

of gentleness and long-suffering'.[30] The activity of loving one's neighbour and *all* humankind is a basis by which one might know that one is assured: it is not an outworking of assurance, but a basis for assurance. Wesley presses this point. To know assurance we must be 'embracing every child of man with earnest, tender affection, so as to be ready to lay down our life for our brother, as Christ laid down his life for us'.[31] It is this activity (along with the activity of loving God) that gives believers 'a consciousness that we are inwardly conformed by the Spirit of God to the image of his Son'.[32] This pattern of thought structurally seems to follow 1 John 4: because God has loved us we are able to love him; and because of God's love towards us, we ought to love one another. Wesley, however, recognizing the distinction between the order of knowing and the order of being, reverses the order in relation to assurance, beginning with the concrete existence of the believer: she may know that she is assured if she loves her neighbour because only God's love is capable of allowing her to do so; if she loves her neighbour, she can know that she is loved of God since God loved humanity before humanity loved God or neighbour.

Wesley makes a similarly structured argument in relation to the fruits of the Spirit. Again, the way in which the believer is able to know the assurance of salvation is through fruits of the Spirit displayed in her life. Only the Spirit can produce such fruit, and so – if a believer produces fruit – that fruit is testimony to the activity of the Spirit in the life of the believer. Thus Wesley writes: 'By the fruits which he hath wrought in your spirit you shall know the "testimony of the Spirit of God". Hereby you shall know that you are in no delusion; that you have not deceived your own soul.'[33] This too is outwards oriented, rather than concerned with the interior life of the believer. Were it not enough that the gifts are displayed and known in relation to others, Wesley makes the point emphatically that he is talking not only about transformed pneumatological personality

---

30 *Sermons I*, p. 273.
31 *Sermons I*, p. 274.
32 *Sermons I*, p. 274.
33 *Sermons I*, p. 283.

traits, but 'outward fruits' – 'the doing good to all men, the doing no evil to any'.[34] This is far from a self-occupied concern with personal salvation: personal salvation is known through a reorientation of one's life away from self-occupied concerns about one's salvation and towards the other.

In one sense, we might think that this concern with fruits ostensibly stands in tension with the teaching about repentance as a sign of assurance, but is that so? There is a sense in which continued calling upon God in confession is precisely a down-playing of the ego that this type of reorientation also describes. In confession, one reorientates oneself towards God's self and away from one's own self; in orientation towards the other and in fruits of the Spirit, one moves from preoccupation with one's sake to preoccupation with the other's sake.

Ecclesial Implications

It may seem strange to deal with what seems on first glance to be a doctrinal locus that operates primarily in relation to the life of the individual believer (in her assurance of salvation) within a volume entitled *Generous Ecclesiology*. However, not only is it the case that (as I have argued) unhelpful forms of as-surance underlay forms of ecclesial operation, but it is also the case that an important feature of assurance for Wesley is the ecclesial context in which assurance is located. For him, assur-ance is not simply an issue for individual believers. He writes: 'And here properly comes in, to confirm this scriptural doctrine [assurance of salvation], the experience of the children of God – the experience not of two or three, not of a few, but of a great multitude which no man can number. It has been confirmed,

---

34 *Sermons I*, p. 283. We should note that, since these are activities of the Spirit in the life of the believer, there is nothing of a works-based righteousness here: the activity of the Spirit in the life of the believer in the order of being pre-cedes the fruits; but in the order of knowing, the fruits are the means by which one might know that one is a child of God. Cf. *Sermons I*, p. 296, and Ralph Del Colle, 'John Wesley's Doctrine of Grace in Light of the Christian Tradition', *International Journal of Systematic Theology*, vol. 4.2 (2002), p. 176.

both in this and in all ages, by "a cloud of" living and dying "witnesses".[35]

The experience of assurance, on which the doctrinal considerations reflect, is one that concerns the whole body of believers – the larger category of the *communio sanctorum*. It is a common and genuinely ecclesial experience that confirms the experience of the individual. But given that the experience of assurance is an internal concern for members of the Church, what has it to do with the 'generosity' with which the current volume is concerned? Here, three points can be identified (corresponding to each of the three features of assurance identified in the section above) regarding assurance in relation to ecclesiological concerns. The sort of understanding of assurance proposed in the above section may offer ways to think creatively and generously about the nature of the Church and its engagement with the world.

Pneumatological priority

The recognition of pneumatological priority over personal assurance is deeply significant. There are important implications to locating both the life of faith and the Church under the third article of the creed and the activity of the Holy Spirit. Centrally, such a prioritization of the doctrine of the Spirit over that of the life of faith determines that it is necessary to reflect on the true condition of the life of faith and of the Church. This true condition is primarily the presence of the Holy Spirit, and not any external set of conditions. The presence of the Spirit is the only true assurance of the present reality of the Church, and not the particular form that the Church takes: there can be no ecclesio-Pelagianism.

This prioritization of the Spirit over the Church is borne out by the testimony of Scripture. In Acts 1.12 we get what *seems* to be the beginnings of the Church. In the Methodist Church, every year the superintendent minister in each circuit reads out the list of preachers; there is something similar with the list of

---

35 *Sermons I*, p. 290.

the disciples in verse 13. We then get a description of worship (v. 14). We have a count of membership in verse 15 (a pastoral roll almost). After that, there is even a parish or church council meeting, with an election of officers (v. 23ff.), and Matthias being elected to a new position. The description of what is going on in Acts 1 looks as though it is a description of the Church. But it is not: what is described is something that only has the semblance of a church. The Church begins in Acts 2, with the coming of the Spirit. The essence of the Church is not in the first instance connected to form. The essence of the Church is ultimately the act of the presence of the Holy Spirit who is present within the variety and plurality of the community in time in all its contingency and diversity.

That the Spirit is the essence of, condition for and basis of the Church should help us to avoid confusing self-assurance with God's assurance; and the reality that the Spirit blows wherever he wills should open us up to be surprised about the forms that the community of the people of God will take. Recognizing the priority of the Spirit may also break down the binary views of salvation and the Church that many hold. The Spirit cuts through such binaries – establishing the Church *within* the world and time and history; working in unexpected and surprising places; forming a visible witness of faith through his invisible presence. Furthermore, the reality that the ultimate condition of the Church is the presence of the Spirit should lead us all to a self-reflective and self-critical engagement with our own senses of self-assurance, and a greater generosity towards other forms of ecclesial practice. After all, Wesley is clear (as we all must be if we live with open eyes in the world) that the fruits of the Spirit are not confined to those who identify themselves, as the Church in various forms does, as *the* 'assured'.[36]

This point about the critical implications that the importance of pneumatological priority brings does not simply apply to those who affirm traditional patterns of Church only: the issue is, rather, that form is only secondary to nature in relation to the Church, and therefore all prioritizations of form over reflections on nature should be self-critical. Indeed, there

---

36 Cf. *Sermons I*, pp. 298 and 310.

is as much (if not more) assurance about who the 'we' are in less traditional forms of Church as there is in traditional forms. And the recent movement towards speaking of the Church in terms of 'incarnational' language concretizes the idea of the Church in unhealthy ways:[37] such language is not only theologically unhelpful (the incarnation is a single and particular event of God at a particular historical moment in Jesus Christ), but also pushes us towards speaking about the substantialization of the Church in people rather than the actualization of the Church by the presence of the Spirit. Through the doctrine of appropriations, it is proper to speak of the activity of God in relation to the Church as being most appropriately spoken about in relation to the third member of the Trinity. The effect of this is that we should be aware of the dynamic and fluid nature of the Church, whose substance exists only because it is founded as an act of the *eternal* Holy Spirit: that is, the Spirit's eternity and holiness assures the temporal continuity of the Church over time, not the particular created human forms of the Church. God does not 'incarnate' himself in the Church; God has already incarnated himself once and for all in the person of Jesus Christ. Instead, God's Spirit founds the Church as a community of his presence, enabling the Church in time to participate in the body of Jesus Christ, to encounter the living and speaking Word, and to be transformed into a community of holiness. This is an activity of God, and not of human form and practice: the Spirit is the *sine qua non* of the Church; the Church is not the *sine qua non* of the Spirit. The children of God need to realize that their assurance both individually and corporately rests on the activity of God, and they should not aggregate to themselves any sense that their own created forms condition the presence of God into resting upon them. This should give the Church a greater generosity in relation to the rest of the world, and it should also make us realize that it is not so easy to identify in a binary way where the Church is: even if we use the idea of logical inference back to the presence of the Spirit that Wesley suggests (see above), as we look around to the rest of the world we will find our categories dis-

---

37 Cf. *MSC*, pp. vii and 8.

rupted as we make inferences about the presence of the Spirit of God in unexpected places.

Humility alongside the world

This breaking down of binarized understandings of the Church in relation to the world through realizing that the Church exists only as an activity of the Spirit of God is also underscored when we consider the first outward identifier of the children of God – repentance. The Church's assurance is not an assurance that exists to raise it over and above the rest of the world; to give it a sense of superiority in relation to the rest of the world; or to enable it to be against the rest of the world. The assurance of the children of God is an assurance that conjoins the Church to the rest of the world: it is an assurance that is expressed in confession of sin, in repentance and in recognition of its continued worldliness. Assurance, resting in the activity of the Spirit and leading to a life of repentance, should create an ethic of humility in the Church, as it realizes that it stands alongside the world, as it confesses its own sinfulness. In this way, the Church is conjoined to the rest of the world, and believers are conjoined to unbelievers: all creation stands in need of salvation, and the Church are those who recognize this as chief among the sinners – those who have the Word of God, and still fail to keep it.

Furthermore, the centrality of repentance to the identity of the assured avoids the tendency to identify a binary demarcated space between the Church and the world, as the promises offered to the Church are promises about the *future*: assurance is something that is felt as *promise*, and thereby is not an assurance of something fully realized in the present. Assurance is in anticipation: it is the assurance of 'things hoped for'. In that way, assurance is only a present experience of the proleptic anticipation of the ultimate.[38] This status does not deny the Church any importance: the penultimate is not only important

---

38 Cf. Dietrich Bonhoeffer, *Ethics*, Clifford Green (ed.), Minneapolis: Fortress Press, 2005; and Bonhoeffer, *Works in English*, vol. 6, p. 168.

in terms of its waiting for the ultimate, but is also important in and of itself. Bonhoeffer writes: 'the penultimate also has its seriousness, which consists, to be sure, precisely in never confusing the penultimate with the ultimate and never making light of the penultimate over and against the ultimate'.[39] Because of the ultimacy of Christ, attending to the penultimate is central. Assurance is important as it points ultimately to the work of Christ in reconciling and redeeming the whole of creation; but assurance itself should not be confused with this ultimate work of Christ. In that way, assurance should lead to a humble identification with the rest of the world, as part of all those in need of salvation. Indeed, for all the importance Wesley attached to assurance, later in his life he became convinced that assurance was not necessary for salvation.[40] For the Church, such an understanding of assurance should lead us to an identification with the rest of the world, and the communities around us, rather than a separation from them: even for the Church, assurance is eschatological; it is for things *hoped for*. The Church should dare to hope for all creation, recognizing in humility its own failings.[41]

Outwards orientation: greatest intensity at fringes

If the gift of assurance is not to separate the Church from the world as those who are saved in contradistinction to those who are damned, what purpose does assurance fulfil for the Church? The purpose of assurance is to free the children of God from preoccupation with personal salvation and the question of one's own standing before God, and to orientate the Church on those other children of God in the world who do not yet know the status they enjoy before the king of all creation. Assurance is not for the sake of the Church: it is for the sake of the rest of the world, as the Church is freed to be Church *for* the world. Here, we are able to see the true direction of God's instrumen-

---

39 Bonhoeffer, *Ethics*, p. 168.

40 *Sermons I*, pp. 200–1; cf. Williams, *John Wesley's Theology Today*, p. 112.

41 Cf. my 'Pessimistic Universalism: Rethinking the Wider Hope with Bonhoeffer and Barth', *Modern Theology*, vol. 26.4 (2010), pp. 495–510.

talization of creation. It is not that the rest of the world is an instrument by which the Church might know that it is saved; rather it is that the Church is an instrument by which the rest of the world might know its standing and status as the creation of God. The Church exists for the rest of the world; the rest of the world does not exist for the Church.

The implications of this ordering of instrumentalization determines that the greatest intensity of assurance that the Church has is found not at the visibly clear centre of the Church (in its services, institutions, offices, etc.), but at the fringe and circumference of the Church, as it meets the rest of the world. Because the Church only exists for the rest of the world, it is in those places where the Church is most actively engaged with the rest of the world that the Church is most intensively the Church, that the Church is most assured that it is the people of God. Wesley's insistence that assurance enables the Christian to love *all* creation and *every* person suggests that it is in loving the very breadth of the *every* and *all* that the true assurance of the Church can be found.[42]

Contrary to models of the Church that rest on forms of assurance that are binary, interior and supposedly clear-cut, a church that seeks to understand its assurance as the children of God in line with Wesley's teaching should be one that is concerned with the sorts of false assurance that the goats in the gospel narrative have:[43] those so ordered on themselves that they do not recognize Christ as present in the rest of the world; those whose binary divides places them in a precarious position before the judgment of God.[44] In the end, the assured are those who are so consumed with loving the rest of the world that they are able to be unconcerned for their own salvation, and are instead oriented on serving the world and seeing it as the world created, sustained and being brought to redemption by God. The Church needs to become the community of the

---

42 Cf. *Sermons I*, p. 274.

43 Cf. *Sermons I*, pp. 281-2.

44 For more on this, see my 'Beyond the Binary: Forming Evangelical Eschatology', in Tom Greggs (ed.), *New Perspectives for Evangelical Theology: Engaging with God, Scripture and the World*, Abingdon: Routledge, 2010, pp. 153-67.

sheep in Matthew 25, who think that they are goats because
they have so loved the world around them that they have not
realized it was God they were serving all along, and yet who,
in loving creation so much, have treated those others as they
would have done had Christ been in their midst. Such a Church
can be assured of the salvation offered to the children of God;
such a Church rests on a form of assurance founded by the
Spirit's work, who opens the Church up to the present activity
of God in the world.

7

The Church as Christ's Holy/Sick Body: The Church as Necessary Irony

ROBERT THOMPSON

The vision for the contributions in this volume can be found in the hope that the debates within the Church of England about ecclesiology and mission, which have been generated by the publications of *MSC* and *FTP*, should not become polarized. In that sense the very term 'generous' encapsulates a difficulty with the *tone* in which *FTP* presents its arguments *against* the vision of *MSC* and its many children, and some of the responses to that critique, which have tended to the adversarial. Such an arch pitch of criticism and counter-criticism is probably not conducive to a fair, balanced and honest assessment of the missionary developments that are envisioned as necessary in the engagement of *MSC* with contemporary culture. Nor does such an arch tone allow for a similarly fair appraisal of how the traditional and inherited practices of modern church life, defended by *FTP*, enrich or impede mission and growth.

The term 'generous' then calls us to a less trenchant style of debate around these issues and seeks to open up a space in which the various voices may be listened to, and engaged with, in Christian charity. The main danger in some of the excesses of the debate is in the splitting in the common body of the Church between those of us who seem all too readily able to cast stones at one another's glasshouses, forgetting that in fact we inhabit the same hot house and in the process break our own glass. Jesus' words, as recorded in Matthew's story of his life, have much to commend them in tempering our debate and dialogue: 'Or how can you say to your neighbour, "Let me take the speck out of your eye", while the log is in your own eye? You hypocrite, first take the log out of your own eye, and then you will see clearly to take the speck out of your neighbour's eye' (Matthew 7.4–5).

Paul ratchets up Jesus' sentiment even further: 'Therefore you have no excuse, whoever you are, when you judge others; for in passing judgement on another you condemn yourself, because you, the judge, are doing the very same things' (Romans 2.1). So I present my assessments of *MSC* and *FTP* within that framework which sets before us God as the one who judges us all, and who will in the *parousia* bring all our imperfections and disunity into the glorious concord of the Trinitarian life. I hope this means that even when I am being most critical, that that criticism is 'generous'.

My own concerns about the tenor of the debate arise from my personal history and ministerial context. First, there is my family background in the north of Ireland. The religious components of the modern history of that part of Ireland make me very conscious, and wary, of any form of polarization, bigotry or sectarianism within Christian communities. Second, in my own ministry I have worked over a range of contexts, reflecting different implicit ecclesiological assumptions, and with a variety of colleagues with whom I have had different degrees of theological convergence. Third, my main appointment at present as the full-time Lead Chaplain of a Multi-Faith Team in a large inner-London NHS Trust places me in quite a different ministerial and missional place than the authors of either volume take for granted. As the Bishop of London's Coordinating Healthcare Chaplain I retain oversight for this particular form of 'sector' ministry across the Diocese of London. Fourth, at the same time, I work actively as an Honorary Associate Priest in a United Benefice of two parishes within the Kensington Deanery which function according to a fairly traditional parish model of ministry.

This diversity of ministerial context and development is probably only really possible within the wonderfully strange and polymorphous ecclesial communities such as can be found within the breadth of the Church of England. That is something which we need to rejoice in and to guard, for it is a heritage that may be our distinct gift that we offer the universal Church. I have found working across that diversity both challenging and enriching. In my curacy I worked with an incumbent with a very different, much more 'traditionally catholic' working ecclesiology and theology of ministry than my own. From him, and from that community, I was blessed to learn the pastoral, compassionate and eucharistic heart of any priestly vocation within the Church of God. This was a context that is probably as close to the ideal parish community, that *FTP* seeks to defend, as can be found. In my present position the bulk of my Christian colleagues, both paid and volunteer, also have working ministerial theologies different from my own, this time in a more 'charismatic' and 'evangelical' way. From them I have been blessed to learn a new reliance on the Spirit of God who energizes and transforms and is not overly constrained by precedent or tradition. This is a context in which the 'parish' already functions in a way that embodies much of the philosophy of *MSC*, with an emphasis on numerical growth and church planting.

Many of my theological college contemporaries, as well as parishioners from my curacy, may well be very surprised at the extent to which I work at present both very closely and productively with Anglicans of a 'different sort'. Such engagement reflects the fact that I have worked in a 'sector' ministry setting for nearly 12 years. Such location requires an extent of collaboration with diverse ministerial and volunteer colleagues which is so much greater than what I perceive to happen between parishes within deaneries or larger ecclesial units. That truly saddens me for it means that there is so much that we are failing to learn from one another. But it is consonant with the semi-sectarian forms of residential training that still dominate priestly formation within the Church, and the propensity of all of us to label others rather too readily. This internal labelling within the Church of England reflects attitudes that are also prevalent within the universal Church and society at large. One of the great privileges of working within the 'secular' setting of a public institution in an NHS Trust Multi-Faith Chaplaincy Team is that quite a lot of our default and knee-jerk labelling is called into question on a daily basis. I lead a team in which we work daily in active ecumenical and multi-faith collaboration to pursue the common goal of the religious, pastoral and spiritual care of our patients, staff and relatives. Questions of what we are able to do across denominational and faith boundaries are always live, often energizing and sometimes tense.

In short, I find myself, in my present ministerial appointments, at once on the margins of church life in 'sector' ministry (one in which I also find myself strangely semi-detached to a parish at its mission-shaped cutting edge), but also embedded in what is still central to the life of the Church in a parochial setting. It is from this experience of a very diverse setting of ministry that I wish to highlight a number of issues that I therefore feel are understressed and underdeveloped in my reading of *MSC* and *FTP*. The first of these is that we live in *an increasingly (religiously) pluralistic nation*. This requires missionary ecclesiologies that offer greater degrees of flexibility in how we understand the Church's engagement with contemporary British life. Second, there is *the centrality of the person of Jesus*. I argue that our theologies of the Church and mission need to be more firmly grounded in the breadth of the biblical witness of the Church to the 'historical' Jesus. Arising from this, third, I will highlight *Jesus' embodiment and teaching of divine compassion*. I believe that we need to recover Jesus' example and teaching on compassion as constituting the heart of the mission of God in and towards humanity, the heart of the gospel. Fourth, I argue that as a Church we deal with diversity in relation to the three significant issues of *prayer, gender/sex and money* in very different ways. We need to learn to be more pluralistic and less self-interested in what it is that we are 'generous' about. In conclusion I wish to present the image of *the Church as Christ's Holy/Sick Body* as central to ecclesiological and missiological self-understanding. It's an image that reflects the healthcare setting of my own ministry. But it is offered as a means of ensuring that Jesus' vision and practice of compassion is at the heart of self-critical 'generous ecclesiology' for the Church as a whole.

An Increasingly (Religiously) Pluralistic Nation

Working in a hospital context means working in a 'secular', public institution in an ecumenical and multi-faith team. I, as an ordained Christian priest, within the traditions of the Church of England, am also the manager for chaplains from other Christian denominations and other faith traditions. As such, every day I not only come across people of other religious persuasions but am, as part of my role, in active dialogue with them in order to fulfil our common task of the religious, pastoral and spiritual care of all of our patients, relatives and staff. The experience of Multi-faith Healthcare Chaplaincy Teams witnesses to ways in which faith communities can work for what is in their common interest, both pastorally and also at a strategic national level. Increasing numbers of marriages in the United Kingdom are 'mixed-faith', and in times of particular human crisis there is a need to address this pluralism and increasing fluidity of religious identity. Both *MSC* and *FTP* need to be augmented by fuller accounts of how their respective visions of mission relate to the faith diversity found in contemporary Britain.

In *MSC* this is, incredibly, wholly absent. My suspicion is that it is absent because the implicit theology of religions that arises from its dualistic construction of the Church and the world would, if explicitly stated, be extremely unpalatable for far too many both within and outside the Church. If God is not in the world, God is therefore not to be found in any other form of religious expression apart from the Christian Church. *MSC* offers an implicit form of religious exclusivism and sectarianism that is extremely problematic for the engendering of good relationships in civil society between people of all faith and none.

FTP offers only a few references to how the celebration of the geographical parish can help to build relationships with other communities in the area. In this sense, its implicit theology of religions is neither exclusivist nor sectarian. However, *FTP* presents a worrying construction of the historical relationship between Israel, Jesus and the Church. In chapter 6 of *FTP*, 'Recovering a Theology of Mission and Mediation', we read: 'In the Acts Pentecost festival we see the action of the Spirit effecting a new human unity, and superseding the limitation and duality of the Law as defining and embodying human relation to God.'[1] The human family is here envisaged as being 'reconstituted'. Part of the authors' positive assessment of that reconstitution is that women are included in the worshipping community, whereas only men would have a place in the Jewish festival of Pentecost. This quotation and line of argument begs a number of questions. The language of supersession is explicitly used. This is deeply concerning in that it unmasks an uncritical, unreflective and triumphalist doctrine of the Church that has explicit anti-Jewish connotations. This is extremely problematic in a post-Holocaust world in which we should be more acutely aware of the ways in which historical Christian anti-Judaism was, and still is, used for anti-Semitic purposes.

The Centrality of the Person of Jesus

What is missing in supersessionist ecclesiologies is Jesus himself. There is not any exploration in *FTP* (or indeed in *MSC*) of the content or tenor of Jesus' teaching. Nor is there an assessment of how novel or otherwise that teaching was from within the plural historical traditions of first-century Judaism. There is hardly any 'historical' Jesus in *FTP* at all, yet alone any encounter with the very alien, first-century, peasant, Galilean, Jewish one, in whom the Church believes we experience the fullness of God.

In contrast, *FTP* paints a Jesus who is safely locked within a fairly ahistorical conception of the Church which we are told, repeatedly, *is* his body. In its reliance on a supersessionist relationship between the community constituted at the 'Acts

---

1 *FTP*, pp. 120–1.

Pentecost festival' and Israel, the Church is favourably depicted as a new, wonderful and inclusive community that has super-seded a law-bound dualistic and patriarchal Judaism. Going back in time it is as if the prophetic tradition of Israel never existed and did not inform Jesus' own religious and spiritual growth and vision of the fullness of the Reign of God. Going forward in time it is blind to how that great gender inclusion of Acts breaks down into the implicit misogyny of other parts of the biblical literature of the New Testament, and its explicit manifestation in the succeeding history of the Church.

This unhistorical and uncritical assessment of the relation-ship between Israel and the Church does not bode well for *FTP* giving us a more inclusive theology of contemporary Jewish people, yet alone people of any other faith. This, in turn, means that it does not offer the resources required for constructing a positive assessment of contemporary multi-faith Britain, nor for the vocation of the Church of England to be the 'Church of the nation', a vocation that *FTP* wishes to retain.

Jesus' Embodiment and Teaching of Divine Compassion

Jesus himself, and his practice of and teaching about com-passion, offers us just such a possible theological resource. Working in a hospital context, ministry is very obviously pas-torally focused on the care and visiting of the sick, ministry around the time of dying and death, with the odd occasional baptism, confirmation and even blessing of marriages thrown in. Working in a 'secular' and public institution means that any form of mission as proselytizing would be inappropriate. This raises live questions for some of my volunteers, many of whom have a vision of mission simply as the making of non-Christians into Christians. In the training of our volunteers we try very hard to broaden this construction. This training con-sists of a series of Bible studies that allow an encounter with the life and teaching of Jesus and a reflection on how this should inform our ministerial practice in the hospital.

The main text that we use is the Judgment of the Nations

in Matthew's Gospel (25.31–46). The radically unsettling nature of this text is not to be underestimated. Increasingly I find that many of our volunteers simply have not reflected long or hard on what the implication of this passage, and others like it, may be for their understanding of who Jesus is; what constitutes his vision of ministry and mission and the Reign of God; and therefore what the connections are between 'being saved', being a Christian, and being incorporated into Christ's body the Church. Jesus' story sharply undercuts all religious polarization, bigotry and sectarianism both between 'parties' within the Church, but also in how the Church is to relate to those who are not part of its own community. What is still truly disturbing in Jesus' parable is that the sheep and the goats are separated not because they did or did not convert one person from one religious identity to another, but simply on the grounds of whether or not they did or did not show compassion. In our training we use much more material from the synoptic narratives of Jesus' life to the same end. The point we want to make with our volunteers is that Jesus judges our Christian discipleship, and therefore our ministry in the hospital, simply in terms of whether or not real human need is met with real human care, compassion and concern.

Building on that emphasis on the centrality of compassion we also want to shake up our too often dualistic constructions of the Church and the world so that compassion is not seen as a dish that we serve up to a hungry diner. This dualistic sense of mission is very often expressed in a hospital chaplaincy team in the idea that as visitors on the wards we are bringing Christ and the gospel to other people and thereby showing them God's love. This attitude often finds expression in pre-visit prayers: 'Father, we want you to be with us so that we can show your love to those who don't know you and so bring them to Christ', or something similar, would not be untypical. What is missing here, for me, is a vibrant doctrine of creation that sees God's goodness in all that is made in God's generous outpouring of God's-self into the heavens and the earth.

In short, then, when more attention is paid to the full range of the biblical literature, and more focus is given to Jesus Christ and his practice and teaching, two issues arise in relation to ecclesiology and the theology of mission. The first is that the centrality of compassion in Jesus' life and teaching means that pastoral care should constitute the very heart of the mission of the contemporary Church. This is because the biblical literature of the Church, which tells the story of Jesus, records this as the heart of God's mission in and to the world in and through his person. Second, the fact that Jesus' practice of compassion is characterized by its radical non-sectarianism means that pastoral care as mission needs to be envisioned not only as the work of building up the body of the Church, but as the work of the body of the Christ in caring for the neediest and most vulnerable and marginalized in our, and God's, world. Just as Jesus' practice is not constrained by Israel's borders, nor should ours be by the Church. This means that a robust doctrine of creation needs to be present in any consideration of ecclesiology and mission, for God is always, already present in his creative and energetic plenitude outside of the body of Christ which is the Church, in the world that he has made.

In relation to the first of these points, *MSC* in its main document has really nothing to say about pastoral care at all. It does not really fit into its focus with church growth in numerical terms and the propagation of new forms of 'being Church'. On the second point, *MSC*, as *FTP* rightly critiques, does not really have a doctrine of creation at all. That's really quite frightening. It's frightening because to omit a doctrine of creation is to construct a religious sectarianism that is unable to see the activity of God outside of our own communities and unable to encounter the face of God in any face that is much different from our own. The irony here is that *MSC* in opening up 'generously' to new forms of missionary activity in the contemporary world actually fails to offer a way of assessing how God may be in those forms 'out in the world' in the first place.

In contrast, *FTP*, in defending the traditional parish and what it has to offer, begins a retrieval of the centrality of pastoral care within the Church's conception of mission. That vision of the parish is also one in which God's goodness is seen in all that God has made and in which mission is constructed as seeing what God is already doing in the world and joining in. However, its focus on the liturgical character of the Church does leave me feeling slightly worried that its primary vision of Christian discipleship tends more to an assessment of how well the priestly hand can swing a thurible than how compassionately it can touch another human person in need. Personally, I love swinging thuribles and censing altars. But, stealing a line of thought from Jesus in the Gospels, the point here is that religious practices are not to be regarded as ends in themselves. The censing of altars points us towards the holiness of God that is revealed in Jesus' offering of his entire life to God and to others, and which culminates in his death, resurrection and ascension. God's holiness is revealed in God's brokenness in Christ's body, which – to return to Matthew 25 – is a brokenness that is encountered in others. The thurible should be seen as Christ's call for us to care for sick bodies.

Prayer, Gender/Sex and Money

But to swing my thurible back on myself, and to be more 'generous' to the authors of *FTP*, what their volume rightly highlights is the old thorny issue of what it is, in such a broad and diverse Church as ours, that actually keeps us together. They focus on the parish system and on liturgy and lament the abandonment of the common inherited traditions of the Church to the consumerist ecclesiology they see as offered by *MSC*. I share much of this concern with them but wish to locate it in a different context.

From my 'secular' setting of the NHS what is very striking is how as a Church we deal very differently with issues of prayer, gender/sex and money when it comes to missiological innovation. The *MSC* culture has effected an abandonment of much of our spiritual heritage to the end of embodying the 'content' of the gospel in a more sellable contemporary 'form'. Such neglect has been accepted by the Church at large as a necessary diversification of ways of 'being Church' in order to bolster mission. However, at the same time, such diversification of church practice in relation to gender and sexuality and suitability for orders of ministry is very lacking. Indeed, some of the intense voracity of those debates may well be attributable to the fact that we no longer share as much common ground in relation to either parish ministry or liturgy and prayer, so that issues of ministerial order take on an inflated importance that they really cannot carry. The debates within the Church about these issues from my work perspective seem so arcane and outdated that I believe that, unless we see a greater generosity from all of us to allow a more pluralistic practice of ministerial order, the Church is in real danger of disregarding the most important issues that really do affect its mission in our contemporary society. The mission of the Church will be severely inhibited because when the increasing popular perception is that the Church does not uphold either the full dignity of women or of LGBTi people, it will find it progressively more difficult to be heard when it addresses the gospel to other pressing ethical issues of our contemporary life.

This is fleshed out for me in my own experience of the NHS and Equalities and Diversity legislation, and of the group of hospital chaplains for whom I have some oversight. In relation to Equalities and Diversity legislation the Church needs to be able to work collaboratively with NHS Trusts to ensure that the provision of healthcare takes account of the religious views and needs of the patient. But at present we also need to be prepared for increasing tension between the Church, as the provider and licenser of healthcare chaplains, and NHS institutions, which actively promote gender and sexuality equality. In my own diocese this has already had a real impact in regard to employment and human rights issues arising in the case of the episcopal licensing of a transgendered chaplain. The increasing divergence between the Church's position and those of our public institutions on these issues calls into question, from both a conservative Christian perspective and a 'secular' one, the morality of the Church being allowed to be in partnership in such a way with our significant public institutions.

For many chaplains, including myself, this is a live, personal issue. In ordained 'sector' ministry in the NHS the proportions

of those of us who are female or who are self-identifying LGBTi
people is greater than in the clergy at large. Within the group of
chaplains for whom I have pastoral oversight the most common
reasons given for this are that within the NHS there is both security of contract and an experience of protection from active
discrimination in the workplace. These are forms of security
that many have not experienced within the Church. For many
of these chaplains, the exercising of their priestly vocation
within a public institution has constituted liberation for them
from a Church that too often fails to treat them equitably or,
worse still, can be experienced as oppressive. In this sense, the
'secular' public institution is perceived by many of us who are
LGBTi as embodying values more consonant with the heart
of Jesus' teaching about, and his embodiment of, the Reign of
God. Or to put it another way, for many LGBTi priests in sector ministry there is always a very clear – and indeed difficult
– tension between Christology, ecclesiology and eschatology.
MSC does not really address any of these classical categories
of Christian theology at all. *FTP* rightly points out how devoid
of any real theological reflection that volume tends to be.
However, *FTP* offers us a collapse of these categories into one
another and so relieves us of all tension. In *FTP* Jesus is the
Church and the Church is the kingdom. If that were the case,
many of us, and indeed many who may be attracted to a more
realistic and honest self-understanding of the Church, would
simply, on moral grounds, not choose to be Christian at all.

But although issues of gender and sexuality will become increasingly important for the missiological effectiveness of the
Church it is the issue of money and the poor that should be at
the heart of any 'generous ecclesiology'. The more centred we
become on the biblical witness to the practice and teaching of
Jesus about compassion, the more conscious we will be that
Jesus calls us in the Church to an equitable sharing of all that
has already been given to us as a gift from God (and which
therefore is in some sense not really ours at all), with the poorest, not only in our Christian communities, but in the wider
society. So while we focus issues of our unity around gender
and sexuality and the episcopate, the biblical model of the Acts

of the Apostles (2.43–7), in contrast, focuses the unity of the Church on the practices of common prayer, common table-fellowship and common possession. Jesus himself in sending the twelve out on their own missionary activity (Mark 6.4–14) tells them to 'take nothing for their journey except a staff; no bread, no bag, no money in their belts; but to wear sandals and not to put on two tunics'. A truly biblical, evangelical and mission-shaped Church would probably spend more time investigating the financial affairs of episcopal candidates!

These biblical visions of the constraint of personal possession in order to share with one another for the common good resonates with our national debates about taxation and the provision of public services and my focus on Jesus' embodiment of compassion. From my NHS context we are now experiencing the most extensive reforms of the health service since its creation. The recent gradual marketization and privatization of healthcare has been accelerated by the Health and Social Care Act (2012). While some degree of competition may well make NHS Trusts leaner and more effective, there is a real question mark over the extent and the quality of care that can be given by businesses that simply aim to make profits. Under such market forces it is the care of the poorest and the most vulnerable in our society that will be most affected. Older people and those suffering from mental health issues often present multiple problems that are very expensive to treat and do not necessarily lead to a 'positive outcome', let alone a positive return on a balance sheet. They may well simply be worse off under the private than the public sector.

But if Christian contributions to these live healthcare debates are not to be easily dismissed as hypocritical, then we also need to look at how we govern our own common life. We need to connect the issues of care and the financial resourcing of the Church's own ministry and mission. The Church cannot effectively speak out about the excesses of under-regulated forms of capitalism in society at large unless it is a community that cares for one another in its own common life and offers a counter-cultural location to rampant consumerist self-interest. At the very least that means that we need to be extremely careful that the forms of Christian faith that we live out and teach are not in themselves individualized, privatized and depoliticized. But it also means that we need to cultivate a greater appreciation of those involved in ministry in the very poorest areas of our country. Our common life should therefore be reflected more clearly in how we raise our Common Fund which needs, in many dioceses, to be more biblically redistributive in principle. We also need to learn to see ourselves not as offering different competing brands of Anglicanism for the contemporary 'religious consumer'. Individual churches also need to learn not to use their own resources as a way of wielding power in the Church that simply apes rather than critiques late modern capitalism. It's on the issues of consumerism, money and the poor that the critique of *MSC* in *FTP* really needs to be heeded.

Conclusion: The Church as Christ's Holy/Sick Body

In conclusion, then, I offer the image of *Christ's Holy/Sick Body* as forming the heart of a 'generous ecclesiology'. To remember that Christ's body is sick is to be recalled to the centrality of compassion and pastoral care as the main characteristic of God's mission in Christ to us and ours in Christ to the world. Second, it is also to remember that the call to compassion that is central to Christian mission is not unique to our religious tradition either, and that this remembrance opens up a space for a more positive theology of religions. Third, it is to reclaim the Jesus whom we meet in the synoptic traditions as central for the Church's self-understanding. To reclaim that tradition is to reclaim a vision of the Church not as indefectible, but which in its very foundational documents offers a story about how truly limited and incorrect (we) the disciples actually are at understanding who Jesus really is and what the gospel is all about. In chapters 8 to 10 of Mark, Peter and James and John are always getting it wrong. We, with them, want a Christ without a cross, a Christianity without suffering, a hierarchical church structure that apes the world and gives us more prestige and better pay and in which some are greater than others. Like these disciples, we too are sick in how we sometimes follow Jesus Christ, sick and in need of healing. That is not just about individual disciples, but it is also about parish communities and the institution at large. Ask any victim of child sexual abuse at the hands of an ordained priest about how sick both individual Christians and the Church can actually be. The Church is a sick body in need of Christ's healing too.

Which brings me to the second part of my title: the Church as 'necessary irony'. A generous ecclesiology that keeps alive the tension between Christology, ecclesiology and eschatology must see the Church as both necessary but also in need of continual transformation into what God intends it to be. It is both holy and necessary in that it is within the life of the Church that the story of Jesus Christ is both remembered and lived out. But it is in need of transformation because in the very remembering of that story we encounter the one who offers us a critique of all religious institutions and their hypocrisies and whose death is, in part, attributable to the outcomes of that critique. The Church keeps the memory of Jesus alive and attempts to live his life in the present in the power of the Spirit. But Jesus' story is a very inconvenient memory indeed and Jesus is such a nuisance to sit with, listen to, deal with and respond to for he continually unmasks just how hypocritical, petty, crass and plain wicked much of what constitutes church life actually is.

It is at the point of fraction in the eucharistic liturgy that we should be most fully conscious of the *Church as Christ's Holy/Sick Body*. The presiding, ministerial priest takes the bread, which is Christ's body, and breaks it, so that all can share in Christ and be brought together in unity with Christ and one another. It is a point in the liturgy that undoes the many prevalent romantic theologies of the Eucharist, ministry, priesthood and the Church. Here, the priestly action reveals the violence that is inherent even within the president and by extension the 'holy' people of God, the royal priesthood that is all those baptized into Christ's identity. The Church, at fraction, is revealed not to be already the location of some realized heavenly peace, nor as the place in which cycles of violence are short-circuited and terminated. Rather, the ministerial priestly action reveals the way in which our priesthood in Christ both overlaps and remains distinct from his. Christ comes as both priest and victim in the self-offering of his own life to God and to others. In the eucharistic drama that self-offering is made present and alive by the Spirit, and that conjoined identity as priest and victim is represented by the presiding priest's actions. But at fraction we are made fully aware that *it is we who break Christ's body apart*, not just in eucharistic ritual, but in the form of the real bodies who in our sinfulness we assault and violently 'kill' in the daily course of our lives. That God whom we violently kill reveals the extent of divine generosity in forgiving our sinfulness and in resurrection returning to us and offering us communion in the Trinitarian life. A 'generous ecclesiology' must be similarly robust about both our personal and corporate sinfulness, and equally assured of God's super-generous forgiveness. With such conviction we will be able to more fully embrace and celebrate the diversity of our own Church and work to make that Church, and the universal Church, more fully reflect the utter generosity of the fullness of God's reign.

8

Inclusive Catholicity

JONATHAN CLARK

'Catholicity is not ... an attainment, so much as a quality of mind; it cannot be possessed, but it can be hungered after. It is not the opposite of anything, except of opposition and exclusiveness.'[1]

If catholicity is the opposite of exclusiveness, the Church Catholic is the Church inclusive. But the Church can only be inclusive because, and to the extent that, God is inclusive. It is not a second-order issue, an optional extra that can be taken up by some and left by others. It does not relate only, or immediately or at root, to the current issues at debate in the Church, especially the Church of England; it is the same question that gave force to the credal debates in the early Church – what are the boundaries of the Church? And how do they relate to the promise of salvation? How inclusive or otherwise the Church should be is a question that concerns us all in relation to our own faith, and concerns all those who believe that the Church's faith is good news for the whole world.

The inclusivity of the Church is not about church politics, whichever church. In the Church of England, it's not about the admission of women to the episcopate or equal treatment of people of different sexual orientations. To the extent that the debate becomes focused on those issues we can be prevented from thinking through in any depth the crucial question. We get caught in the confusion of different preconceptions and prejudices, for instance in relation to gay or lesbian people,

---

1 H. H. Kelly SSM, *Catholicity*, London: SCM Press, 1932, pp. 32–3.

which make it more difficult, not less, to have a real debate, even a meaningful disagreement. Those on either side of the debate know already where they stand, and have no hope of persuading the other party, so arguments are posed positionally and rhetorically rather than in an effort to seek the truth together.

There are two compelling reasons to try to get beyond the presenting issues and think in general terms about how inclusive the Church should be as such. First, it enables us to deal with this subject with the seriousness it deserves. This isn't, as some allege, just a contemporary liberal social issue masquerading as theology – it is central to our self-understanding as Christians. And second, by moving on to this theological ground, we may be able to move away from our combat positions and be able to listen to and learn from one another. That of course does imply that those (like myself) who stand on the inclusive side in the Church's struggles might have something to learn – might have to change. It also involves facing up to the mixed evidence in the Christian tradition and in the biblical books, not just choosing the parts that suit us. In what follows, I write from my own perspective; I hope that those who come to the issues from other standpoints will find the principles applicable in their own theological reflection.

Exclusive Inclusivity

So let us begin by reminding ourselves that God does not always send out the most inclusive messages, in the more common sense of the term. 'You shall have no other gods but me', 'I the Lord your God am a jealous god' are good examples of that dominant strand in the Old Testament books that emphasizes the exclusiveness of the worship of Yahweh – that it cannot be combined with the worship of the other gods of the ancient Near East, and that all sign of their worship is to be extirpated.[2]

---

2 I am noting, but not entering into, the question of when this belief developed during Israel's history, and how the books might or might not reflect the historical course of events.

That exclusiveness does not go away. 'No one can serve two masters', says Jesus – the call to follow God remains incompatible with any other obedience. The Church was built on the blood of those who refused to compromise their Christian faith through worship of the Roman emperor. One of the fears of those who distrust the word 'inclusive' is that Christian faith will become just another lifestyle choice, part of the repertoire of beliefs that may be logically incompatible, but happen to fit an individual's emotional needs at one particular moment. In our individualistic and consumerist society, that is a reasonable fear – it would be very easy for faith to become exactly that. Those of us who are happy to bear the 'inclusive' label need all the more to make it clear that we know how radical and all-encompassing is the call to Christian discipleship. We need to show that we are not afraid to speak as Jesus did of repenting and believing in the good news. Any Christian who can see nothing in their social setting that is an offence to the gospel of Christ isn't looking very hard; to be an inclusive Christian does not at all mean going along with whatever the majority think. To give one immediate example, an inclusive stance towards refugees and asylum seekers in the United Kingdom at present has to involve a critical stance towards the actions of our present government, and its predecessor, and a challenge to the general consensus in society.

There is a radical exclusivism at the heart of Christian faith. But – and this is one of the characteristic paradoxes with which our faith abounds – there is an equally radical inclusivity, and it is seen most clearly on the cross. It was explored in the last century by one of the great – and not in the least liberal – theologians, Hans Urs von Balthasar. This chapter can only touch on this, one of the deepest themes of von Balthasar's work, and in doing so I focus on only one work, *Mysterium Paschale* (1970). The more accessible tone of that work is rooted in a theology: 'of a God who is dialogue in his very being, who can be "other than himself" and yet restore himself to himself, who because he can "lose and retrieve" himself can lose and retrieve the world, can lay down his life and take it up again'.[3]

---

3 Rowan Williams, 'Balthasar and Rahner', in *The Analogy of Beauty: The*

In *Mysterium Paschale*, von Balthasar begins to explore this theme not with contemporary philosophy, but with the Fathers. He quotes from, among others, Cyril of Jerusalem:

God has opened wide his arms on the Cross in order to span the limits of the earth's orb and goes on to recall Athanasius' description of Christ extending his arms on the cross to the two people represented by the two thieves, and tearing down the separating wall of division – which itself of course is built on the phrase from Ephesians: 'For he himself is our peace, who has made the two one and has destroyed the barrier, the dividing wall of hostility.'[4]

Von Balthasar goes on: 'Even in its outer form the Cross is inclusive. What shows forth the inner inclusiveness, however, is the open heart out of which is communicated what is ultimate in Jesus' substance: blood and water, the sacraments of the Church.' For von Balthasar, the inclusive love of Christ is also the inclusive life blood of the Church.[5] He goes on to say: 'The opening of the heart is the gift of what is most interior and personal for public use: the open, emptied out space is accessible to all.'[6]

It is on the cross that the exclusivity and inclusivity of God converge: 'the theology of the Covenant, moving towards its completion as the idea of a bilateral contract between God and man, finds its fulfilment in unison with that of the unilateral promise which preceded that concept of Covenant.'[7] God's unilateral act of inclusive love makes possible the complete and exclusive 'yes' which can be the only possible response to that love – the yes that von Balthasar sees in those who remain at the foot of the cross, the nucleus of the Church.

Theology of Hans Urs von Balthasar, Edinburgh: T & T Clark, 1986, pp. 11–34, 32–3.

4 Hans Urs von Balthasar, *Mysterium Paschale*, San Francisco: Ignatius Press, 2000, pp. 129–30.

5 Balthasar, *Mysterium Paschale*, p. 130.

6 Balthasar, *Mysterium Paschale*, p. 131.

7 Balthasar, *Mysterium Paschale*, p. 132.

The Church is that body which responds with an exclusive 'yes' to the inclusive love of God. Its founding members are not what von Balthasar calls 'the church of males, and of office', but 'the church of women ... [and] a church of love at the foot of the cross, represented above all by [Mary] and the "disciple whom Jesus loved"'.[8] This heart of the Church can never be reduced into the institutional Church, but remains both its counterpart and its lifeblood.

This is a radical recasting of the notion of an inclusive Church. The Church is inclusive because it must reflect that same giving up of itself that Jesus accomplished on the cross: 'For the meaning of Christ's coming is to save the *world* and to open for the whole of it the way to the Father; the Church is only a means, a radiance that through preaching, example and discipleship spreads out from the God-man into every sphere.'[9]

The inclusive mission of the Church comes from the sharing with and in Christ that the cross signifies: 'In traversing "the greatest distance" in the act of substitution, Christ includes all people, and enfolds all refusal of God by going to its root. But the unique act of redemption demands in return the act of conversion, that is to say the commitment of human freedom to all others.'[10]

Sharing in suffering with Christ is at the heart of an inclusive Church, so that we may also share in the new life of Christ. For von Balthasar, this is not a purely forensic identification with Christ, but an ongoing experience in the life of Christians and the Church. He is careful, though, to make it clear that this sharing in Christ's suffering is placed within the 'sovereignly free grace' of God's act of love. The suffering Church suffers as the body of Christ, because it is united with Christ its head, not in order to add anything to God's action but to say yes to that action becoming its own.

---

8 Balthasar, *Mysterium Paschale*, pp. 16–17.

9 Hans Urs von Balthasar, 'In Retrospect', in *The Analogy of Beauty*, San Francisco: Ignatius Press, 2000, original German edition Benzinger Verlag, 1970, pp. 194–221, 194–5.

10 T.-M. Pouliquen, 'La substitution inclusive au fondement de la morale chrétienne chez H. U. von Balthasar', *Nouvelle Revue Théologique*, vol. 13.2, 2009, pp. 243–61, 260 (my translation).

The Church is given over exclusively to inclusivity. There should be nothing that remains in us that is not caught up in the boundless love of God for the world expressed on the cross. This is not a side issue or a matter of church politics, but the very challenge of the gospel. We are all asked – what is it that needs to be put to death in us, so that the inclusive love of Christ can live in us?

As the quotation at the beginning of this chapter indicates, the word 'Catholic' signifies for me that very wholeness of the gospel, which is for all people – it is about the catholicity of the whole Church. It expresses the very diversity of ways in which people have responded to the inclusive love of God. It is God who is catholic, because it is God who loves the whole of creation with the same intense passion that we can only feel for a very few. For us to define the limits of catholicism is to pervert the term – the catholic Church is the whole Church of Jesus Christ, demonstrating his love. When Archbishop John Habgood gave a lecture entitled simply 'Catholicity', he ended it thus:

> [I]n the long term, the future lies with Catholicism. It must, because only Catholic tradition is rich enough and stable enough to be able to offer something distinctive to the world without being captured by the world. But it must be a Catholicism which is true to its highest vision, and hence broad enough, hospitable enough, rooted sufficiently in sacramental unity, confident enough in its inheritance to be able to do new things, diverse enough, and yet passionately enough concerned about unity, to be genuinely universal.[11]

This vision of the Church's life can only be sustained by a theology of the Church as deeply rooted as that of von Balthasar, because it challenges at every level our prejudices and, even worse, our sense of justice. The cross is not justice – it is costly love, love that includes even its enemies.

---

11 John Habgood, *Confessions of a Conservative Liberal*, London: SPCK, 1988, pp. 90–1.

The Scandal of Inclusiveness

Having explored an inclusiveness flowing from the cross, and flowing into the life of the Church as the body of Christ in the world, sharing his sufferings, it is clear that any such inclusiveness is likely to be costly. It is costly precisely because it is inclusive, for it sees the catholic Church in so many places. The first and greatest cost to inclusive Christians, I believe, is to include, to love and count as fellow believers, those who do not reciprocate, those who believe them to be misguided or even heretical.

The mystery of the cross, and of God's saving love, is greater than we can hope to understand. If it is impossible to speak the truth of God in any human words – which I think it has to be, if God is God at all – then none of our statements of faith can claim to reveal the truth of God without remainder. There is always more to say. Similarly, none of our ways of worship or church life can claim to be definitive. If that is true, then we also have no grounds on which to denounce those who worship in ways we find embarrassing or inadequate, or who believe things about God with which we disagree. Instead, we should always be looking for those signs of God's grace to which our own tradition or preference may have made us blind.

The Church of England is a particularly rich field of diversity in church life, and my own ministry as a bishop brings me into contact with the whole range. In the few months (as I write) since my consecration, I have already been surprised, challenged and enriched by the variety of church life among the parishes in my care. I have also had to set aside my own ecclesiological preferences in order to lead worship for congregations in a way that reflects their own tradition of faith. I decided early on that I would not seek to impose 'my way'; that my calling as bishop was to lead from within each church's practice and pattern, so long as it was within the capacious boundaries of what the Church of England allows. That experience allows me to affirm from experience what I have been deducing from theological principle – that the catholic nature of the Church is most truly exhibited when it is diverse, not uniform; that common identity does not require conformity of practice; that the Church's mission is strengthened by differences held in love. It is in my view profoundly catholic (in the theological sense) to regard the Church as diminished if it is only Catholic (in the sense of a particular approach to theology and worship).

Our calling as a whole body is to recognize this calling, which is part of the scandal (in Greek, *skandalon*, a stumbling block) of the cross. This demand is certainly one of those that most makes me stumble, especially when I disagree with fellow Christians on profound issues of doctrine or Christian life. Without having to agree, I have to recognize that those from whom I differ are still my brothers and sisters in Christ. Whether or not they feel the same way about me is quite irrelevant. In some way, and I don't pretend to know what it might be, they too are responding to the mystery of the love of God.

In order to conceptualize this theologically, von Balthasar can help us again. He ties together the incarnation and the passion through a consideration of kenosis, Christ's self-emptying which begins with the birth of Jesus and is completed in his death. He suggests that kenosis should not be thought of only in respect of the earthly life of Jesus, but that the self-emptying of Jesus reveals a fundamental aspect of God's nature: 'God is not, in the first place, "absolute power", but "absolute love", and his sovereignty manifests itself not in holding on to what is its own but in its abandonment.'[12]

The jealousy of God for God's glory is turned inside out by the love that empties itself of glory so that it may be shared by all. Christ is always, within the Trinity, that person which exhibits the humility of God, the obedience of God to God. But if our sharing with Christ is real, then the first words of the famous hymn in Philippians become a stark challenge: 'Let the same mind be in you as was in Christ Jesus': kenosis is for us a part of Christian life. We are given the gift of sharing in the life of God, not as something to claim or grasp, but so that we too can serve as Jesus served. That humility must extend all the way. Some of us find it relatively easy to visit the sick and the

---

12 von Balthasar, *Mysterium Paschale*, p. 28.

poor – but less easy to admit that we might be wrong in our thinking. For some it may be the other way round. To admit that there may be some truth in a theological position that we find wrong and offensive is the kenosis of the intellect.

A truly inclusive Church is as inclusive as the cross, not as inclusive as our much narrower understandings of what is proper and right. The cross remains a scandal to us all, because it challenges us to include the improper, the guilty, the defiled. Liberal Christians are often quite happy with that sort of language, because we secretly think it signifies those people that we don't think are improper at all. But it includes not just those the Church has traditionally excluded, but also those who have done the excluding. Although von Balthasar does not go on to spell this out, the suffering to which we are called in the Church may be exactly that unbearably painful stretching out of crucifixion, to embrace those who (we feel) deserve no embrace.

Proclaiming an Exclusive Inclusiveness

The inclusiveness of the Church is founded on our own being included with Christ, in his humility and his suffering. What should we then do, in exhibiting our exclusive commitment to the inclusive love of God? Von Balthasar is clear that our inclusion in Christ is not an act of passive reception, but an act of transformation and of call to mission.

One thing we should definitely not do, then, is keep quiet about the faith we hold. I do sometimes still meet faithful Christians who are giving their heart and soul for the relief of poverty, or the pursuit of justice, but find it almost impossibly painful to admit publicly that they are doing so because of their faith in Jesus. It is true that among young adults in Britain, coming out as a Christian can be about as difficult as it was to come out as gay 30 years ago. The recent film *Trollhunter* made the point in a somewhat acute way. The group of students who find themselves hitched up with the depressed troll hunter are asked if any of them are Christian – because, as the children's rhyme goes in English (in the original version), 'Fe, fi, fo, fum,

I smell the blood of a Christian man', trolls can smell people of faith. The one Christian student is too embarrassed to admit it – and is torn to pieces by the trolls in consequence.

Christians are called to live our faith unapologetically but unaggressively. We are to tell and live the good news of Jesus, always as good news – in every setting and every conversation, the gospel is good news, not bad news. It may sometimes be the good news of a surgeon's scalpel, cutting away what brings death so that life may grow, or more often the good news of healing to the wounds that individuals or the world have suffered already – but it is always a positive statement. We need to find ways of proclaiming the good news of Christ which cohere with this vision of an inclusive Church: ways of telling others about the joy of our exclusive commitment to Christ that are not themselves judgemental or excluding. We cannot forget the many ways in which the Church has in the past, and continues in the present, to be exactly those things: but we can live something different. One of the keys to doing that in my own practice of ministry has been my rediscovery of the plural and communal nature of faith.

In the Church of England's liturgy, after the credal interrogation at a baptism, which uses the Apostles' creed, in which each clause begins 'I believe', the priest says 'This is the faith of the Church' – to which the response is 'This is our faith. We believe in one God, Father, Son and Holy Spirit.' And that is the form in which we say the Creed at the Eucharist – it is a communal affirmation.

Emphasizing the plural nature of the Creed has two consequences that enable us to be exclusively inclusive. First, it places a distance between the faith of the Church and the state of mind or heart of the individual. Belief is about belonging, not a separate category. This bald statement deserves more defence, which it can't receive here, as it brings me straight into contradiction with one of the most popular analyses of religious practice in the UK – the idea that people are more likely to belong to a church than to become believers. For me, this is to fall into the trap of individualism. Christian faith is a communal thing – to belong is already, at some level, to believe.

If faith is the Church's, then we can proclaim it with confidence, without making every individual feel that they need to sign up to every word before they cross the threshold. In fact, quite the opposite: the Church can with confidence welcome the seeker, the unbeliever, the casual wanderer in, and let them if they wish become an integral part of the body, because the faith is the whole Church's, not the sum total of the individual belief of the people who happen to be present.

The Church shares in the life of Christ, who welcomed all sorts of people who might be thought to have compromised his religious purity. But in fact it wasn't he who was overwhelmed – it worked the other way round: his divine life and love overwhelmed what was deathly in those he met. The visible Church – what von Balthasar called 'the church of office' – cannot claim that same fullness, but at its heart is the 'church of love', the Church at the foot of the cross. So whoever it might be that would be thought to contaminate the Church, they can be welcomed.

Inclusivity at the Heart of the Church

I said there were two consequences of thinking of faith as a plural, communal activity, not a singular decision or state of mind. The second is this, and it may answer a question left hanging earlier in this chapter. If we cannot claim to know the whole truth of God, because God is a mystery beyond our understanding – and if we must accept those with whom we disagree radically as fellow Christians – where do we draw the line? If no line can be drawn at all, the Church, one might argue, dissolves into all the other worldviews and religions available in the spiritual market place.

It is the language of drawing a line that deceives us here, in my view. The Church doesn't need a boundary rope – it needs a heart. It is the central identity of the Church that preserves its uniqueness: the identity that is expressed through the exclusive commitment to Christ which allows no other. If that has to be expressed in words, the traditional creeds of the Church provide them, but in reality it is expressed through the worshipping and serving lives of Christian people and communities.

It is in the tension between these two that the Church is discerned. There are some with whom I find it very difficult to establish a personal connection: I don't feel as if we share the same faith. But if they will say the same creeds with me, I have to start from the presupposition that we do. Similarly, there are some whom I instantly relate to, with whom I have a natural bond which for me is distinctively Christian – but they are reluctant to talk of creeds or specific beliefs (the Quakers are an obvious example in the United Kingdom). Similarly, whether or not I am intellectually sure, I have to accept them as fellow believers. This leaves a fuzzy and uncertain margin, a contested one, maybe also a more organic one, as befits a body. It will always enrage those who desire clear and unambiguous answers, but it seems to me to reflect more of the inclusive/exclusive tension, by holding both aspects, than any answer that comes down on one side or the other. It makes it difficult and painful when decisions have to be made that do exclude, and that is right, because such decisions should not be easy.

It is the very openness of an inclusive Church that provides a platform from which the exclusive demands of Christ can be articulated without being perceived as imperialistic or judgemental. When it is clear that no one is rejected or denigrated, the challenge of Jesus can be exactly that – a challenge to a new way of living that is also pure gift. The Church has no need or call to denounce those who live another way; its task is to speak out with passion and conviction about its own calling. The Church's articulation of that calling has to be made with as much humility as passion: each local church community – indeed the Church as a whole – only continues to live the life of Christ if it is made up of pilgrim people, who always recognize that God calls us beyond what we have yet been or seen. The call of Christ can only be authentically made by those who know their need of continuing conversion.

A Pilgrim Church

What von Balthasar describes as 'the church of office' is both inevitable and dangerous for the Church. For him it is typified by Peter, the one on whom the institution of the Church is founded – and the one also who abandons Christ at the crucial moment. Even without the same identification of Peter with the Church, we can recognize the same dynamic at work in every institutional church. The Church as institution is always in danger of betraying Christ through substituting its own agenda for the gospel. Not that it is done consciously or deliberately; boards and committees composed of faithful and spiritual men and women can between them create oppressive and life-destroying structures that none of them wishes or personally intended.

An inclusive Church is always an unfinished Church.[13] The four traditional 'marks' of the Church are that it is 'one, holy, catholic and apostolic'; I'm not arguing against those criteria, but I would also like to suggest that they should, as a post-structuralist would put it, be placed under erasure. That is to say, in saying those things we must recognize also that the Church is in fact plural, fallen, squabbling and inward-looking. The pure moment of the Church of love can only be remembered through the institutional Church, but it must also continually be there challenging the institution to remember that it does not exist for itself.

Some people assume that an inclusive Church has no use for the tradition, and pretty little interest in the Bible. Certainly, it's true that the people of God, in biblical times and after, have often excluded those for whom Christ dies, and believed they were doing God's will when they did so. The Church should not airbrush out its shameful history, but confess it: we do after all believe in the forgiveness of sins. But there is another, more profound story that leads in quite a different direction, and it is that story which can enable the Church to grow into inclusiveness. It is the story of tradition as something unfinished, as the

---

13 This section is indebted to Steven Shakespeare's and Hugh Rayment-Pickard's *The Inclusive God*, London: Canterbury Press, 2006.

story of the continuing work of the Spirit to lead the people of God beyond our natural and sinful desires to exclude and to dominate.

It is a story that starts from the inclusiveness of the cross, and traces that inclusiveness both backwards and forwards. It traces its roots back to the creation, to God's blessing of the whole good creation God had made. With Paul, it emphasizes that call given to Israel by the prophet Isaiah not to exist for its own sake but to be a priestly nation for all the nations. It tells again the story of the Church's beginnings, recognizing the struggle and conflict that led to the inclusion of the Gentiles – as Gentiles – into the people of God. It brings out the stories that became hidden as the early institutional Church developed – the stories of a Church that welcomed women in leadership, which made no distinction on ethnic or social grounds between its members.

That is the tradition in which the Holy Spirit has been at work, not the tale of tradition that sees the Church as always and everywhere perfect, and incapable therefore of change, because any change from perfection must be a loss of perfection. It is this view of tradition that can provide a way of tying together very different approaches to church life, of the sort that are now in the Church of England often labelled Fresh Expressions. To try to escape from the Church's institutional framework is both futile and harmful. Futile, because another institution will inevitably grow in its place; harmful, because the tradition of the Church has within it the potential for its own transformation. New movements within the Church recall the whole Church to 'the church of love'. They do so all the more deeply if they are themselves rooted in the tradition of a Church called to renew itself for the salvation of the world, and not for its own concerns.

If this is the Church's story across time and space, the resources of Scripture and the tradition are not closed, or opposed to the insights that come from the Spirit's action in new Christian communities. It is the Church's job to bring all those insights together into a conversation that is also the process of discerning God's work in our place and time. This process of discernment enables the people of God to grow in maturity and confidence on the pilgrim way. While rooted and grounded in the tradition of the Church, we remain open to what the Spirit is teaching us through contemporary insights. As together we read the Scriptures, worship and pray, and live out our faith in the world, we are playing our part in the evolution of that tradition itself. But it's not a tidy or monolithic tradition – it has both the life, and the unpredictability of a living organism.

A living and developing tradition can be a place in which we are allowed to experiment, and allowed to get things wrong. Because we know that we are never in possession of the whole truth, we have to keep on exploring, and learn from one another's experiences. That provides us with a model for mission and worship, and a command always to act in context. The exclusive inclusiveness of the gospel sets us going, and the tradition provides us with a history and a direction, and the Spirit guides us in the present into the future: but none of those add up to a set prescription of what it means to be the Church in a particular time and place. It will always be different, if we are really discerning, because every place has its own needs and opportunities.

I began by saying that the inclusivity of the Church must reflect the inclusivity of God, and I've tried to indicate the dimensions of the challenge for us as Christians as we seek to do that. I'd like to finish by remembering that the path leads in both directions. We are welcomed by God's love, which is without reserve, and must therefore live out that same love to the world. In so far as we do manage to live God's love, we are also opening the path for others to know God. That is the purpose of the Church, not its own continuation, but that the world may know and be able to respond to the love of God. We are never perfect in that task. In the end, as Pope John XXIII wrote, 'God's mercy is our only merit.'[14] That is as true for the Church as it is for each of us in our own lives.

---

14 Pope John XXIII – 'Last Will and Testament' – 29 June 1954, www. catholic-forum.com/saints/popeo261j.htm (accessed 23 September 2012).

Afterword: The World
and the Church

IAN MOBSBY

The gap between critical approaches to Christianity and the simplistic spirituality promoted in lots of churches lies at the heart of so much disillusionment with Christianity today. Many long for an expression of the Christian faith that reconciles heart and head, that offers a positive, engaging spirituality that is also committed to grappling honestly with difficult and painful questions, and that longs to make the world a better place.[1]

The content of this book is a brave and important contribution to the debate bordering on rant between the supporters of the *MSC* versus *FTP*. Broadly speaking, this has been marked by those whose sensibilities and theological understandings start in different places – between those who start with the context of the world, mission and the kingdom of God, and those who begin with being the people of God, the ecclesial body of Christ, the Church. This divide has been characterized by the instinctive reaction of whether to be conservative or progressive in response to the challenging and increasingly post-secular situation the Church finds itself in. Further, this division has become a gaping wound exacerbated by different church traditions where an 'either-or' binary has been created between the two great theologies of the Christian faith – redemptive versus incarnational theologies. The generous challenge, then, of this book is to intentionally explore how we avoid the over-

---

1 Dave Tomlinson, *Re-Enchanting Christianity: Faith in an Emerging Culture*, London: Canterbury Press, 2009, p. 5.

simplicity and violence of dualistic thinking, and establish together how we do mission, *and* be the Church holding on to both redemptive *and* incarnational theologies. This is a massive task requiring the Church to be 'joined-up', and there is no one answer, but it is urgent. How do we define what is important? How do we rally the depth we seek in the Christian faith regarding being the Church *and* engage in informed mission practice without defining ourselves in opposition to those we do not agree with? In the recent history of the Church of England we have not been good at non-dualistic thinking, where both the low/protestant/evangelical and the high/sacramental/catholic traditions have both defined themselves in hostile reactionary difference. The health of our Church, theological thinking, prayer, worship and mission depends on us avoiding dualism with a focus on Christ's New Commandment to love the body of Christ in a unity that accepts diversity and with a Church that is *in* the world but not *of* it. In fact, you could argue that the Great Commandment, the highest point of Jesus' teaching, has to be the ultimate non-dualistic calling or vocation for the Christian – to love and worship God, and love your neighbour no matter who they are and how they offend you, in the context of the world. A Church that defines itself in opposition to the world – and this includes contemporary culture, which is not a godless void – is not living out its *sentness* through the apostolic nature of the Church in obedience to God's *Missio Dei*. As Harvey states: 'Christian communities must learn to deal with the problems and possibilities posed by life in the "outside" world. But of more importance, any attempt on the part of the church to withdraw from the world would be in effect a denial of its mission.'[2]

At the same time, we do need the more mission-minded not to *dumb down* on the marks of the Church and the importance of its sacramentality and worship; to realize that, if we do so, this will effectively impoverish our mission. We do need to enable and train Ordained Pioneer Ministers and others to be custodians of the worship traditions of the Church, and this

---

2 B. A. Harvey, *Another City*, Harrisburg: Trinity Press International, 1999, p. 14.

includes an earthy and grounded understanding of the sacraments and sacramental practice. The increasing numbers of the 'de-and-never-churched' are a call for Church to be much deeper, relevant and spiritually nourishing, and our mission in the world as the arena of the kingdom of God to be culturally relevant *and* true to the faith.

What I am not hearing in this book so far is just how much things are stacked against the more mission-minded in this debate, for which the Fresh Expressions initiative has been a great liberation regarding permission, support and recognition. For too long mission practice and the study of missiology have been seen as the poor illegitimate cousins to church–parish pastoral practice and the study of ecclesiology. This book generously seeks to rebalance this imbalance of power and influence, which we can trace as the vestiges of the privilege of Christendom. If we learn anything from the Oxford Movement, it is from the stories of just how hard it was then and is now to be listened to and taken seriously regarding mission and wanting to do something new. Listen to the many voices who in the nineteenth century, could not get adequate permission to re-found religious communities for the many who felt called to a renewal of the vocation to the religious life led by an obviously mission-minded Holy Spirit. Luckily for us the powers could not hold back the floodgates of God's intentions. It was the lack of a generous ecclesiology and missiology of parish priests, archdeacons and bishops of the Church of England that made this so difficult.

I welcome both Bishop Jonathan's and Bishop Stephen's chapters, as I suspect a more prayerful, inclusive, mission-minded and prophetic understanding of the episcopal vocation would have helped at the time of the Oxford Movement. I too am excited by Bishops' Mission Orders and how they will enrich the diocese and deaneries as Anglican expressions of the local church. Nothing is more exciting and envisioning than when bishops take informed and prayerful risks, and share prophetic wisdom. We so need theologically informed, passionate and prophetic bishop-pastors rather than the pressure on them to be administrative chief executives. I also want to affirm Julie

Gittoes's chapter and the metaphor of the 'Wandering Church' of the people of God on a pilgrimage carefully walking in the world. This feels like an important corrective to the 'Church as static institution', which counters the triumphalist and at times idolatrous understanding of the Church. Such metaphors bring the Church alive as a dynamic and living body or event, shifting back from impersonal institution to community. I like the resonance here with Brutus Green's reaffirmation of Augustine's *saeculum*, where the Church has a humble and loving connection to the world. As Brutus hints, there is much in our post-secular contemporary culture that is hungry and searching for transcendence; the question remains whether the Church is willing to engage in the ordinary lives of people who will not go to their parish church because they find it inaccessible and alien.

Finally, I want to mention the elephant in the room of much of the writing of this book, and it is the sphere of contextual theology. The conservatism of *FTP* concerns me because the position being supported believes that we do not need new disciplines, we just need to do theology properly.[3] I could not disagree more and I suggest the exploration in Chapter 3 makes this implicit. It will never be an easy task to hold in tension church tradition, theology, the Bible, cultural change and the particular context you are theologizing in, without a commitment to non-dualism and the need for tools to assist us. For example, the work of S. B. Bevans on *Models of Contextual Theology* is a crucial, thorough and joined-up way to explore such a difficult task. His writing around the transcendent model of contextual theology has much to say about authentic missional and evangelistic engagement with our increasingly postmodern and post-secular contexts. These *new* disciplines aim to be academically rigorous and seek to assist Christians engaged in being church and doing mission practically. Disciplines like models of contextual theology also show the strengths and weaknesses of different approaches. In our post-Christendom world, we can no longer rely on not

---

3 This does not just apply to contextual theology, but also to pastoral and practical theology.

considering context more fully. This is not some 'liberal pursuit based on bad theology' as a proponent of 'Radical Orthodoxy' once challenged me, these are tools that seek to empower effective engagement with the world, seeking not to be on the one hand imperialistic and colonialist and, on the other, not syncretistic. In so doing, we utilize tools to help us achieve Robert Thompson's five generous engagements in Chapter 7. I hope that readers of this book will prayerfully wrestle and question their thinking and practice through this book; and finally and importantly, I finish with the prophetic words of David Tacey, which need a generous place to be heard fully:

> What if it [the Church] ignores the present challenge or does not care enough to take up a dialogue with the world? The yearning for sacredness, spiritual meaning, security, and personal engagement with the spirit are the primary needs and longings of the contemporary world. What is happening if the institutions of faith are so bound up with themselves and resistant to change that they cannot make some contribution to these needs? Our contemporary situation is full of ironies and paradoxes. Chief among these is that our secular society has given birth to a sense of the sacred, and yet our sacred traditions are failing to recognize the spiritual potential.[4]

---

4 David Tacey, *The Spirituality Revolution: The Emergence of Contemporary Spirituality*, London: Brunner-Routledge, 2004, p. 20.

Index